IS IT SAFE TO DIE?

What Others are Saying...

Is It Safe to Die? may be the most gripping book you ever read.

A depressed, bitter, angry atheist, Kat Dunkle was given a second chance at life after dying on the operating table and was told to come back and share what she'd learned with others. That mandate led to writing this book detailing her near-death experience.

Is It Safe to Die? is a comprehensive no-holds-barred account of Kat's traumatic life before her NDE and her remarkable transformation since then. If you ever thought your life was hopeless or that how you choose to live it doesn't matter, then you need to read this book.

If you are not a believer, the inspirational message in this book may make you rethink your relationship with the Divine."

Bruce Greyson, M.D.
Professor Emeritus, Psychiatry and
Neurobehavioral Sciences
University of Virginia
Author, *After: A Doctor Explores What
Near-Death Experiences Reveal About Life and Beyond*
Author, *The Handbook of Near-Death Experiences*

This wonderful book tackles the sensitive subjects of loss, grief, and the persistence of God's love. The author's near-death experience inspires those who feel hopeless to switch to hope, those who feel faithless to switch to faith, and those who feel loveless to switch to love.

The author is the perfect example of someone who has walked this path of darkness and come to realize that the light of God's love never, ever leaves us even when we are not our best selves.

KIMBERLY CLARK SHARP, MSW, LICSW

AUTHOR, *AFTER THE LIGHT*

FOUNDER, *SEATTLE ASSOCIATION FOR NEAR-DEATH STUDIES*

It is my honor to recommend *Is It Safe to Die?* to you.

Living in this fallen world as a believer presents challenges each day. Keeping our sights on Jesus allows us to survive and, on occasion, bring along others.

Kat has struggled more than most. Reading how she has gained the strength to endure gives us hope!

JERRY RIESS

MISSIONARY TO ROMANIA

CALEB MINISTRIES, WWW.CALEBGOODNEWS.ORG

This memoir written by Kat Dunkle is compelling as she tells her story. At times the trials and difficulties she endured seem unbelievable yet are pure truth.

I've known Kat for over ten years and have been blessed to watch how her life has glorified God more and more each day.

DANA RAUSCH

AUTHOR,*SHAVING OFF HIS MANE: OVERCOMING THE HABIT OF DEVALUING YOUR HUSBAND*

Through the toughest life challenges Kat shares about in *Is It Safe to Die?*, Kat came to understand that the only safe place to live was in surrendering to Jesus Christ and living as a Spirit-filled believer with a strong ministry mindset.

Kat has a great appreciation for God's grace and mercy and a strong conviction that everything she has been through, including her near-death experience, has prepared her to minister to others and share the good news of Jesus Christ with those who will listen.

Kat understands the brokenness of the human condition and how poor choices can take a toll on a person's life. Her heart in writing this book is to direct people to know Jesus as personal Lord and Savior, experience God's presence, and live for God's purposes rather than the empty pursuits this world offers.

PASTOR DAN JOHNSON

WESTSIDE FOURSQUARE CHURCH, BURIEN, WA

Is It Safe to Die?

A Memoir of Death-to-Life, Second Chances, and Redemption

Kat Dunkle

KD Publications

K D PUBLICATIONS

Published by Kat Dunkle Publications.
ISBN 979-8-218-06215-6

Edited by Jeanette Windle at www.jeanettewindle.com.
Cover designed by Hina Shakti (Hennah) at www.99designs.com.
Book interior, final format, and ebook designed by *Ebook Listing Services* at www.ebooklistingservices.com.
Contact the author at thekat137@aol.com.

DEDICATION

With all my heart to my loving "ever after" husband Don Dunkle and my three incredible sons Chris, Dusty, and Mark.

TABLE OF CONTENTS

ACKNOWLEDGEMENTS

Thank you to author and friend Kathy Collard Millar for all her encouragement and advice during the writing of this book.

Thank you to my editor Jeanette Windle who put the words all together.

FOREWORD

by Kathy Collard Miller

Far more than just a near-death experience (NDE), this powerful memoir by Kat Dunkle is an incredible story of transformational death-to-life. I first met Kat more than twenty years ago. When she told me of her NDE, I was intrigued but a little skeptical as I'd never personally known anyone who had gone through such an experience. But the unwavering and vivid consistency of her account and passionate zeal for sharing it with others soon convinced me she was telling the truth. Even more convincing was her deep faith in God and genuine walk with Christ.

What Kat survived long before her NDE makes this incredible story of an ascent to heaven, descent to hell, and redemptive second chances even more glorious to God. None of us are made completely whole the moment we come to know Jesus as Lord and Savior. And Kat's story isn't just about the astonishing events of that fateful day when God arranged for her to die—and be restored to a changed life.

It's about God healing her from an abused childhood and abusive first marriage. From her own journey into alcohol and self-destruction. From the pain and grief of losing her young son in a tragic death accident. From bitterness, anger, and rebellion against God along with so many other horrible things Kat has endured.

That's why I'm so excited that Kat's story is now available as a book. It will minister to every person in some way. You'll read about loss, grief, abuse, doubt, evangelism, studying the Bible, and transformed thinking. You'll get lost in a story so mindboggling you'll be tempted to think it is a novel with a fantastic plot and intriguing characters.

But this is no novel. It is a real, vulnerable, and very intimate peek into someone's actual life. As with all good stories, the reader will identify with the protagonist's challenges and rejoice with her triumphs.

More deeply valuable than that, this compelling page-turner is an inspiration for every reader who longs to draw closer to God and has wondered if God's power can help them through their own difficult life challenges. Kat's memoir drew me closer to God, and I know it can do the same for you. I urge you to see how God wants to minister to you through this powerful book. I believe with my whole heart that you won't regret it.

Kathy Collard Miller

Award-winning author of *The Daughters of the King* Bible study series, *No More Anger: Hope for an Out-of-Control Mom*, and *God's Intriguing Questions series*.

Introduction

Is It Safe to Die?

Life can be a harrowing experience for everyone. Growing up in the 1940s and 50s with an unloving father whose job had us constantly moving around the country left me with many insecurities and feeling different from other kids. I escaped from a difficult homelife into a bad marriage, becoming a mom of two sons by the time I was twenty-one years old. Divorce, poverty, and depression plummeted me deeper into self-loathing.

Then on a blind date, I met a wonderful man, whom I married less than a month later. Another beautiful son came into my life. My husband and I started a business. As far as I was concerned, my life was close to perfect.

One thing this life didn't include was any relationship with or belief in God. Though I'd attended church in early childhood, God had hardly crossed my mind in over fifteen years. I had seen so much pain and cruelty in my own life and the world around me. If God really existed, then He must be to blame for allowing such pain and cruelty. So I preferred to reject any possibility that God existed.

Then devastation hit. My middle son was killed at just seven years old. The business my husband and I had started went bankrupt. My father dropped dead of a heart attack. All within a few months. From that point on, my perfect new life and marriage began unravelling. I grew increasingly bitter and angry. Above all, at any thought that a God might exist who had allowed my precious son to be taken from me at such a young age.

Through a combination of circumstances, I ended up in the hospital for emergency surgery, where I flat-lined and was declared clinically dead. While the period in which I was clinically dead may have been quite brief in earthly terms, what I experienced during that time seemed far longer and was excruciatingly intense. I was first given the gift of feeling God's presence. Then *all hell broke loose* as I plummeted into a horrific pit of darkness and burning pain filled with anguished screams of other lost souls. I knew without a doubt that I was plunging into hell and that it was my own fault for having rejected God.

Amazingly, my heart started beating again, and I came back to life. Why did God let me come back? The one thing I now knew for certain was that God, heaven, and hell were all real and that I'd been given a second chance. While still clinically dead and undergoing that horrific experience of hell, I'd cried out to God, asking for forgiveness and redemption. The last thing I remember before coming back to living was the voice of God saying, "Bring people to Me!"

Life drastically changed after my death-to-life experience. God healed me physically, mentally, emotionally, and spiritually. He healed my marriage and brought my husband and children to faith as well. He also gave me a clear vision for founding a business in a field never tapped before. I became the focus of numerous magazine and newspaper articles on women in business.

Since then, I've gone on to be a speaker, Bible teacher, and business consultant as well. I've been interviewed for multiple television documentaries and books focused on near-death experiences. I believe each of these opportunities were part of God's directive to me while still clinically dead to "bring people to Me."

It is for this same reason that I am now writing my story in full. I write this book for every reader who has suffered loss of any kind. Loss of a loved one. A career. Even your own life. I also write for every reader who may be suffering bitterness and anger due to loss, hardship, trauma, abuse, and depression. Or perhaps your life appears to be going well now, but you've chosen to reject the existence of a loving God because of past pain and grief.

If you are reading these words, then know that God loves you and is calling you this very moment to Himself. I invite you to accompany me on my own death-to-life journey in these pages. As you do so, it is my prayer that you too will seize that second chance, place your faith in a loving heavenly Father, and walk with Him daily.

And when your day should come to leave this earthly life behind, as it comes to all of us, may you have absolute certainty in your heart that it is indeed *safe to die* and that you will live for eternity with God in all His glory.

Is It Safe to Die?

CHAPTER ONE

FALLING INTO DARKNESS

The tiles on the hospital ceiling went flying by as I looked up at them from my prone position on a gurney. Masked people rushed alongside me. Confused thoughts whirled through my mind. *Who are these people? They must be doctors. I don't even know them. Can I trust them?*

My life was out of my control. Decisions were being made for me by total strangers who seemed to disregard the questions I was asking and my obvious anxiety. As I was wheeled toward an operating room, I felt completely helpless and terrified. *Am I going to die? Will I ever wake up again?*

Then I felt the comforting touch of my husband Don's hand on my shoulder. I heard him address the surgical staff anxiously. "Please stop! Please let me speak to her!"

He leaned over me, his crystal-blue eyes looking sad and defeated. Softly, he said, "I love you."

I shut my eyes, my heart beating out of control. Love me? I was convinced my husband no longer even liked me, let alone loved me. I'd been so sure I'd finally found my one true love. But now my storybook life was disintegrating into ashes. My memory relived the horrible fight we'd had. A fight that had landed me in the hospital and on my way to surgery.

My whole body shook as the gurney was wheeled through the door of the operating room. The bright lights blinded me, and I felt like I was standing naked on a stage with a spotlight highlighting every flaw. I heard a woman's voice comment snidely, "Can you believe she's just in her twenties?"

"You'd never know it!" another voice snickered.

I knew I must look terrible, and I felt so embarrassed that all these people were standing around looking at me. Just moments earlier, I'd been lying in a hospital bed talking to my husband when three men with white coats had rushed in. I assumed they must be doctors.

"Kathy, we suspect you have internal bleeding," one of them said gravely. "And we have to find out why. We're going to need to take you into surgery immediately."

"No, no, I don't even know you!" I responded in a panic. I always thoroughly researched any doctor I consulted, never blindly trusting anyone's advice. So why would I put my life in the hands of these total strangers?

"I'm sorry, but this can't be delayed any longer," the white-coated man responded firmly. "We have to find out why you are losing blood. You also need to tell us just how you got that bruise on your back."

I knew exactly how I'd gotten that bruise, but I was too embarrassed by the answer to speak. I lowered my gaze to avoid their probing eyes, hoping they wouldn't ask again. But I knew my silence was just arousing their suspicions. Would they think Don had tried to kill me? Would Don get in trouble? Would they call the police?

They won't understand how our emotions exploded in the car. How I attacked Don while he was driving. Yes, he swung out and hit me. But it was anger on both our parts that brought us here.

In the months since my precious seven-year-old son Mark had been hit by a car and fatally injured, the once-loving relationship between my husband and me had become very stormy. We seemed to live in a never-ending cyclone of emotions, arguing constantly. My heart was still shattered by Mark's death. But I also carried the guilt that I hadn't been a good mom. After all, what son should die before his mother? I was supposed to protect him.

All I wanted in life now was to be alone with my memories of Mark. I couldn't socialize with people and didn't even want to try. That evening I'd been furious with Don for insisting we leave the house to attend a gathering of friends. As he drove us toward the party, we once again began quarreling. The argument escalated quickly. Don was telling me I needed to move forward from Mark's death. I just wanted him to shut up.

Move forward? I will never move forward. All the pain and fury that had built up within me since Mark's death exploded to the surface. Reaching across the bucket seats of our car, I lashed out, my fingernails tearing into Don's face and my fists delivering blows.

"I hate you! I hate you!" I screamed.

I didn't really hate my husband, but I was like a can of gasoline just sitting ready for someone to drop in a lit match. With his insistence about putting my son's death behind me, Don had dropped the match. What I truly hated was the circumstances but even more so myself.

Don struggled to pull the car over to a stop at the side of the road while fending off my attack. As he maneuvered the steering wheel with his left hand, his right hand swung out at me, striking me so hard on my back that I saw stars exploding. I fell back into the front passenger seat, sobbing hysterically. I was left both mentally and emotionally devastated as well as in physical pain.

As I thought back in response to the white-coated man's query, that single angry, wild blow from Don was the only possible explanation for the bruise that so concerned the doctors. But how was I to explain the circumstances? That Don was protecting himself from an out-of-control wife? The horror and pain we'd been living with since Mark's death? Fearful they wouldn't understand, I chose to ignore the men's question about my bruise.

I had now been moved from the gurney to the operating table. An anesthesia mask was placed over my face. Moments later, darkness began closing in on me. The sterile operating room grew dim, and all the surgeons and nurses faded from sight.

What's happening to me? I wondered frantically. *I should be unconscious. I can't breathe. I'm struggling. Am I dying? I have to breathe.*

The frenetic activity and rapid voices of the medical personnel that had filled the room moments before were now gone. Instead, I found myself completely alone in an eerily quiet and dark place. I was still fighting with all my might to breathe, but I just couldn't.

I feel like I'm drowning! Somebody please help me! I'm suffocating!

Suddenly, the terror that gripped me vanished and was replaced by an overwhelming, unbelievable peace. I was now moving forward very slowly down a darkened passage as though I was traveling down a birth canal about to be born into another realm. I stopped struggling, fear and dread replaced by curiosity. *This is so strange! I don't have to breathe anymore. Where could I be?*

Far below me, I caught sight of my husband and sons. They were huddled together and appeared to be crying. I knew they were sad because I'd left them and wanted to let them know I was all right. But I was already drifting further along the darkened tunnel.

I floated past four other people I didn't recognize standing together in the same darkened passage. They were dressed in street clothes so were clearly not medical personnel. I wondered why they were looking at me with such somber, apprehensive expressions as though some sort of doom was about to befall me. Just as I passed them, I felt a very strong nonverbal transmission or communication go through my mind. It was far more than just a thought. It was a knowing. *There is no God!*

These were the words I'd convinced myself of for years, the belief I'd made a deliberate choice to accept as true. But just then I was shaken by a piercing, howling, deafening roar of sound. Simultaneously, I felt the physical sensation of a massive cord ripping painfully through the middle of my body as though it were burning right through my flesh. It moved so fast I could glimpse what appeared to be smoke rising from it like some out-of-control locomotive thunderously, violently infiltrating my flesh.

Then in an instant, the burning, ripping sensation and noise stopped, and all uncertainty was erased. *There is a God!* It was as though the terrible roar of sound and painful ripping through my body had seared all my unbelief right out of my being. Without any lingering doubt, I knew that I knew that I knew that I knew God really did exist.

The result of this instant revelation was astonishing. I can't even describe the peace that came over me. There was no fear, pain, anxiety, or concern at all. Those negative emotions had been completely replaced by a total understanding of how truly glorious God is. I was experiencing the perfect peace of God, and it was magnificent.

In truth, there are no words that come even close to describing what I actually felt. This was not a dream. If you placed your hand in front of your face, could anyone else convince you it wasn't there? I knew this was happening, that God had allowed all this to happen, and I never wanted to leave His presence.

Then once again in an instant came the piercing, deafening noise. The burning, tearing sensation ripped through my body. Once again, a non-verbal transmission entered my mind, telling me what I'd convinced myself for years to believe. *There is no heaven!*

But as before, the revelation suddenly came to me without any doubt. *There is a heaven!* I knew that I knew that I knew that I knew this heaven was a literal place where people spend eternity in union with God, experiencing this wonderful, magnificent peace and knowing they will be in a state of perfection with God forever.

Thanksgiving filled my heart as I contemplated an eternity free from any negative emotions or thoughts or fear. No more death or dying or sickness. No sadness, boredom, or rejection. A place filled instead with light, love, goodness, contentment, and holiness. Excitement overwhelmed me as I felt myself drawn toward what appeared to be a door with a sunburst of light shining around it.

But right at that moment, the horrendous noise came again, howling through me like a hurricane. The burning cord seared through my flesh. Another non-verbal transmission filled my consciousness. *There is no hell!*

This was one belief I could have wished to hold onto. But I immediately started plummeting downward, falling into total darkness. A horrible, endless space completely void of any light surrounded me. It was darker than a night without stars, dark as the complete blackness of an underground cavern. Imagine you are standing in an elevator and the floor suddenly disappears, leaving you spiraling downward totally out of control. Can you even imagine the horrible, helpless feeling of falling and being unable to stop?

I was not only terrified of the tumbling fall through the darkness but enveloped in the agonizing pain of burning. There were no flames, only pain engulfing my entire body. All around me, other anguished screams combined with my own terror-filled shrieks as we fell together into oblivion.

There is a hell! I now knew this without any doubt and that the pit into which I fell was hell. I was gripped by the hopelessness of knowing I would be there for eternity. The certainty that there was no escape from the macabre nightmare. I wouldn't wake up or hit bottom and die. I wouldn't be rescued by anyone. I would fall and burn in this gruesome pit forever and ever and ever.

Just moments before, I'd felt myself within the grasp of heaven and eternity with God. Now I'd gone from the sensation of knowing God's wonderful, perfect peace to falling into the horrendous pain and destruction of Satan's dark abyss, reserved for those who disregard the Creator of mankind and defined by total separation from God.

Even worse was the knowledge that I'd somehow sent myself here. This was all my own fault. God hadn't done this to me. I'd done it to myself. I'd had a lifetime to prepare for this very moment, and instead of choosing to believe in God, I'd chosen to turn away from God. I'd chosen my destiny, and now it was too late to cry out for mercy and forgiveness.

Or was it?

Chapter Two

Yet to Be Written

All people have the desire to believe in something. As a child, I blindly believed in God. I also believed in Santa Claus and thought the Tooth Fairy was real.

I know now that belief in God's existence was placed within my heart from the beginning. In fact, the Bible tells us that an innate knowledge of God is planted in every human heart (Romans 1:19-20). But as I grew up and life became blurred, faith in God also became something blurred and unreal that I no longer believed any more than I believed in Santa Claus, the Tooth Fairy, or all the rest of the lies I'd been told.

I was born in August 1942 in Portland, Oregon, to parents who at best were very confused in their convictions and whose relationship with each other was extremely contentious. My father had left school in the sixth grade to support his widowed mother. During World War II, he'd served in the Navy on the aircraft carrier USS Saratoga. After the war, he took a job with the Department of Agriculture, working his way up the ladder to a respected position as a government meat inspector.

Despite good pay and a secure position, my father hated his job. He dreamed of being his own boss and owning his own business. He even had a friend who offered to partner with him in a restaurant. My father so wanted to take that opportunity. But he felt stuck, or so he thought. He now had the responsibility of a family to support, and he felt that he couldn't leave the security of his government position to step out into an uncertain world as an entrepreneur of a business that wasn't guaranteed to bring in a good income.

His friend went on to start the restaurant on his own, which in time became famous in the area. He became very wealthy and was eventually elected mayor of the town where he lived. My father never got over his friend's success and his own dashed dreams. Thoughts that he could have been equally successful made him bitter, and he blamed his wife and children for holding him back. I understand now that neither the small girl I was then nor my mother and siblings were responsible for my father's choices. But at the time, we were made to bear the guilt for his disappointments.

It didn't help that my mother was a college graduate with a pharmacy degree. She was the only woman in her graduating class at Oregon State University and a pioneer as a woman stepping into male-dominated careers, which the pharmacy field was in the late 1930s. In that place and time, women were rarely given such opportunities.

In my memories of my parents, I could always sense tension between the upper-class, sorority-queen college graduate who was my mother and the elementary-school-dropout, rough-and-tumble, angry man who was my father. They never spoke of how they'd met or became a couple, so to this day I have no idea what brought them together. I could only assume she'd been attracted to the strong, masculine, war-hero serviceman he must have seemed when they first met. I didn't realize the class difference between them because my mother always worked hard at portraying the perfect family, happy and normal.

From my father, I absorbed the lesson that if you choose the safe path and don't follow your dreams, you're going to be miserable, so you should just go for it and live life to the fullest. From my mother, I learned that women could enter into areas of business or education and become successful, however strange that might sound since her own success was consigned to oblivion due to my father's jealousy.

In total, my parents had four children. Their firstborn was a brother one year older than me. I adored him, but for some reason my father hated him. Hate is such a harsh word, but no other word describes how this brother was abused as a child by my father. Many times, I asked my mom why, but she couldn't or wouldn't answer me. My younger brother came along five years after my own birth and was greatly cherished by my father. The baby of the family, my little sister was born when I was ten and was revered by both my parents.

In contrast, my older brother and I have few good memories of childhood or of parental love. We saw little of either parent since they both worked, so we were mostly cared for by nannies. When they were home, we were not allowed to bother my father in any way or we would get in terrible trouble. We couldn't play music, talk and laugh, chew too loud at meals, or make noise of any kind. Nor were we allowed to have friends over to play.

Mom excused my father's harshness by telling us that he worked very hard and shouldn't be disturbed when he was resting. That she too worked hard all day didn't seem to matter to my father. Not that my mother encouraged questions either or even just sitting and talking. I grew up thinking all grownups were like this and that our dysfunctional family was normal.

In truth, my parents were two people who refused to accept each other for what they were. This caused constant arguments and power struggles. My father had affairs and was abusive. My mother put on a happy face and turned to alcohol to cope. In fact, alcohol was the only common bond I saw between my parents and played a big role in their lives and our household.

Since I wasn't allowed to speak to my father, I looked to my older brother as my father figure and hero. He was handsome and popular in school, and it was easy to place him on that pedestal. As we were so close in age, I always wanted to be with him.

He in turn was constantly trying to chase me away. I had a little black velvet cloak my mother had made for me, which was lined in red shiny satin. My brother hated that cloak. I would follow him everywhere with that little cloak on.

"Go home, sissy!" he would shout at me. "Quit following me!"

But I would just smile and continue after my hero. Even when he picked up dirt clods and threw them at me, I would call out, "I still love you, Tannie!"

His name was Stan, but in my childish voice it always came out, *Tannie*.

I was small enough I don't even remember any of this. I just loved and adored my wonderful big brother. But he told me decades later how his behavior haunted him and how badly he felt for his mistreatment of me. I just laughed and told him, "I still love you, Tannie!"

In this timeframe of the 1950s and 60s, children were routinely left to play outside until dark without supervision. This was certainly the case for my older brother and me. We drank water out of hoses. We ate icicles that dripped off the roof. We never wore a helmet on a bike. We crossed busy streets on our own and walked home from school. Yet somehow we survived.

On one beautiful August afternoon when I was four years old, I was outside riding a brand-new tricycle my parents had bought me for my fourth birthday. Sitting on my tricycle, I watched the birds flying overhead and marveled at the intense blue of the sky. Just then, a boy about the same age as my hero big brother walked by. Out of nowhere, I felt his hands on my back. Then he shoved me hard off my tricycle.

Boom! I crashed into the sidewalk, hitting my head against the concrete. The boy immediately came over, putting on a contrite expression.

"Oh, I'm so sorry, little girl," he exclaimed, offering me his hand. "Here, let me help you."

I rubbed my head, feeling so confused. Scrambling to my feet, I slowly got back on my tricycle. To my shock, I felt the boy's hands again on my back. Once more, he shoved me, even harder this time. I fell again to the hard cement. Blood was now trickling down my face.

"Ouch!" I screamed, my eyes welling over with tears.

"Oh, I'm so sorry! I didn't mean to do that again. Here, I'll help you." The boy's arms yanked me to my feet. As he did so, my leg got stuck in a tricycle wheel, which sliced open my skin. Blood spilled down my leg. I was so terrified I could hardly breathe as that terrible boy shoved me down one last time, then walked away laughing.

My little heart was broken that a boy no older than my hero big brother could be so mean. But what could I do? Who could I run to? Mom and Dad weren't home at the time. Working, I suppose. I have no idea where our current nanny was. The cut on my leg left a permanent scar that screamed for the rest of my life, "Don't trust anyone!"

Though at this time, I did still trust in God and never even considered He might not exist. Like most children, I just believed. My father never attended church. On Sunday mornings, he stayed home watching sporting events on television. But when she could, my mother attended a Catholic church close to our house. She was fascinated by Mary, the mother of Jesus. It was almost as if she found her own identity and respect in the way Mary was elevated within the Catholic religion to such a high position that everyone admired her. Admiration my mother always wanted but never got.

As a child, I accompanied my mother to church and found much comfort there. The Catholic mass at that time was still in Latin, so I didn't understand much of what was being said. But I loved the scent of incense and the feeling of peace and solemnity. I think it was the only place I really felt safe from the terrible power struggles my parents had with each other. Sitting there inside the church sanctuary, Mom seemed content. There was no arguing.

I also loved the chiming of the huge bells that rang out in the church belltower every day at noon. I would walk over to the church, unsupervised as always, and sit outside on the grass, eagerly waiting for the bells to chime and running my hands over the carved granite statues that decorated the church grounds.

The Catholic church had a parochial school attached to the church property. I was in awe of the children allowed to attend there. I couldn't have been more than five years old when I remember vividly pressing my nose up against the school fence to watch the children playing in the schoolyard at recess. How blessed they were in my little mind to be in a school learning about God. I was too young to know any difference. I just knew what I felt, which was that these were special children, different from me.

In fact, at this point in my young life I yearned to be around the people of God and the things of God. Being in church was one of my greatest desires, and when I was able to go, I never wanted to leave. I longed to be closer to God.

Children are such beautiful clean slates to be written on. Unfortunately, life just isn't all good!

Chapter Three

Stop!

While I had an innate belief in God as a small child, my knowledge of God was only what I felt, and feelings tend to change. I was never taught much about God, so everything I learned was like seed being planted in unfertile ground. My faith was unable to grow.

Also, while the church services and the atmosphere inside the sanctuary gave me a sense of overwhelming peace, I never really knew what was going on. The Catholic mass was in Latin and never really explained, so we didn't learn much about Jesus or God. Lay people were not encouraged to read the Bible. In fact, I didn't even know what a Bible was in my childhood.

My parents did encourage their children to have a religious belief but didn't demonstrate such in their own lives. My father sent us off to church while he stayed home watching television. My mother didn't always go either, especially as we children grew older, but they would made sure we went. I always wondered why my parents weren't in church themselves if it was so important.

Another very negative influence on my faith in God was my paternal grandmother, who occasionally watched us when no other babysitter was available. She was a small, rotund woman who always walked very upright and stiff, chain-smoking one cigarette after another. She expected everyone to jump at her command, and even my intimidating, dictatorial father would jump when his mother spoke. Grandma was very jealous of my mother and would always put Mom in her place, which she considered to be well beneath her own.

In those early years, we always went to Grandma's house on Christmas Eve. I loved Christmas. It was the most wonderful time of my year. The beautiful lights. The Christmas carols. The nativity stories. Candy hung from the magnificent Christmas tree. Presents underneath.

But going to Grandma's house on Christmas Eve wasn't really that fun. My mother would call impatiently, "Kathy, get your coat on! We're leaving to Grandma's house."

"But, Mom!" I would protest. "I don't want to go! We might miss Santa."

When we arrived at Grandma's house, it was always filled with adult relatives and family friends there for the festivities, all drinking, singing, and eating. Cookies, candy, and other goodies were set out on tables. My big brother and I were the only grandkids at that time, so we were banished to the basement where we wouldn't bother the adults. Filling up our plates with anything we wanted, we'd obediently head downstairs. The basement was old and musty. Closing the door so the adults couldn't hear us, we'd eat our fill of goodies, then play tag. Whenever my brother caught me, he would start tickling me.

"Stop it, Tannie!" I screamed. "Stop it!"

That did draw attention even above the noise of the adult party upstairs. Coming to the top of the basement stairs,

Grandma yelled angrily down the steps, "You two be quiet or you'll really get it."

We didn't take her seriously, giggling and making fun of her as soon as she closed the door. Once we thought Grandma was gone, we'd go right back to our games and laughter. Then the door would open again. "I told you two to be quiet. Now you're going to get it!"

She'd come waddling down the stairs, a piece of firewood raised high in one hand to give us a spanking. There was a bedstead down in the basement, and we would scramble under the bed to hide. My big brother always got there first, and he kept pushing me out where Grandma could get me.

No, Christmas was not a good time when it meant going to Grandma's house. But there were other times when going there didn't seem so bad. Grandma was a fortuneteller who read tarot cards, tea leaves, and had a crystal ball. The only time I really liked being around her was when she would take out her crystal ball and tarot cards. We would sit at the kitchen table, where she always had candy for me.

"Kathy, I see a long lifeline for you," she'd tell me. "It's going to be a very difficult life. But you will be loved by many people, and you will marry a very handsome prince someday."

As a child, I was fascinated by Grandma's fortune-telling. I would gaze up at her with absolute confidence that every word she said was an open book into my future.

"Kathy, I am a good witch," she assured me. "And you are my little witch."

This made me feel important because Grandma didn't like anyone. I really thought she could make things come true. I really thought she was a witch. And maybe she was!

My father's government job as a meat inspector entailed being transferred every two years on average. When I was seven, we moved from Portland, OR, to Mount Lake Terrace, WA, a small town not far north of Seattle. Though in general I hated the constant moving, this one was an exciting place to live with beautiful green forest surrounding a small lake.

A collie kennel just down the street from our new home had the most beautiful dogs I'd ever seen. It was owned by a woman whose husband was in the U.S. Merchant Marine, which meant that he was out at sea for months at a time. She bred the dogs for show, so they were amazingly well-trained.

Whenever I had free time, I would run down to the kennel to see the collies. It wasn't long before the owner asked me if I'd like to come inside and pet them. We soon became great friends. I loved helping her feed the dogs and clean their kennels. Sometimes she even let me groom and exercise them. As I walked the collies along the sidewalk, I gave them voice commands, and they obeyed. I felt so important when people stopped to watch me handle the dogs.

The kennel owner also took me with her to dog shows, where I watched with astonishment how the trainers worked these beautiful animals. Afterwards we would come back to her house. She'd make fudge, popcorn, and cookies, and we'd play cards until it got dark. I loved being with her, and life was so happy.

Today's readers might wonder how a small girl could just be off on her own at a neighbor's place without parental supervision. But it was a different era, and children running around the neighborhood until dark was a normal thing. Since both of my parents worked full-time, there wasn't really anyone to notice how much time I spent over there.

Then one day her husband came home from sea. I felt sad because his arrival interrupted the great fun I was enjoying with my friend. One evening, I was feeding the collies as had become my regular routine. I'd reached the furthest kennel when he walked down from the house. The kennels backed onto a stand of tall, wide-branched trees. He strolled far enough into the trees that he was left standing in deep shadow.

"Kathy, come over here," he called out. "I have something to show you."

I didn't like the man, and his dark, shadowed figure under the huge trees seemed somehow creepy. But in that time period, children were taught to obey adults even if they were virtual strangers. Concepts like *stranger-danger* hadn't yet been invented. And of course this was my friend's husband, so I had no reason not to trust him. Reluctantly but obediently, I walked towards his shadowy frame.

When I got close, he grabbed my hand. That's when I realized he'd opened his pants to expose his genitals. Forcing my hand down, he made me touch him. I was both terrified and horribly embarrassed to see a grown man's anatomy, something I'd never even known about at that point. I tried to pull myself free, but he was much bigger and stronger and held me fast.

Then in my struggle, I tripped, falling to the ground. This somehow yanked my little hand out of his. Getting up, I ran towards home as fast as I could, never looking back. My heart was pounding right out of my chest by the time I reached our front porch. Trembling all over and with tears pouring down my cheeks, I raced breathlessly into our house and headed for the safety of my bedroom.

Since this was evening, Mom was home from work. As I dashed by, she called out from the kitchen, "Kathy, what's wrong with you?"

By the time she'd followed me into my bedroom, I was cowering down in a corner with my arms wrapped tight around my knees, rocking back and forth. I felt filthy all over and totally confused. Through my tears, I sobbed out what had happened.

My mother immediately ran to find my father, screaming hysterically. A short time later, he stormed into the house bellowing furiously, "Lola, call the police! I'll show that *!@#$%* a thing or two!"

Mom called the police while I continued to cower dazedly with my hands over my ears, rocking back and forth. Eventually, a nice policeman with a large silver star on his shirt took me downtown in his patrol car to the police precinct. Unlike my parents, he spoke softly, and he wasn't scary like my friend's husband. In fact, I felt completely safe sitting in a big chair alone with this nice man.

"Kathy, you must tell me everything that happened," he commanded gently.

I didn't know the words to describe certain parts of the male body, but the nice policeman told me. He also assured me that nothing was my fault. Still, I felt very shamed and guilty. If I'd just kept quiet and not told my mom, none of this drama would be happening. Even worse, I was afraid my friend would be mad at me for getting her husband in trouble.

Sometime later, the case went to court. I had to testify. Sitting on a huge chair in the witness box, I could barely see over the railing separating me from the rest of the courtroom. A mean man stood there calling me a liar. He told the court I'd made the entire thing up because I was jealous of my friend's husband.

Why is he saying that? I wondered frantically. *Why is he so mad at me?*

Only much later did I realize this man was the defendant's lawyer. My friend's husband was sentenced to a year in prison, and my friend never spoke to me again. For the remaining time we lived in Mountlake Terrace, I was always fearful her husband would get out of jail and kill me. Despite the policeman's kind assurance, I still believed it was somehow all my fault. Why hadn't I just kept quiet?

I loathed men after that. Their smell. Their hairy arms. Even when my father tried to get close to me, I felt nothing but disgust and anger. I had learned the hard lesson that people can't be trusted. And that included my father.

When I was about nine or ten years old, we moved again to Tacoma, WA, a much larger city than Mountlake Terrace about thirty miles south of Seattle on the banks of the Puget Sound. My baby sister was added to our family around the same time. Since I was so much older, I became her babysitter along with extensive household chores such as laundry and cleaning.

By this time, my older brother was routinely running away due to my father's cruel treatment of him. So on weekends when our nanny wasn't there, I became the only real childcare my younger siblings had. Sometimes my parents would leave me to babysit while they went out drinking and partying. A couple days would go by before they returned home. Today this would be unacceptable parenting, and even then I can guess looking back that it was related to their alcohol abuse.

Another move meant another new school. I didn't make many friends there, but one classmate named Sharon was nice to me. One day, I invited her over to my house to play. It was too far to walk, so Sharon took a bus, also quite normal for young children in that time period. We had a great time laughing and playing together outdoors.

But it was getting dark, and Sharon needed to catch the next bus home. Reaching into her pocket for her bus money, she discovered she was a nickel short. We both panicked a bit as the bus was already coming down the street. Then I came up with a solution. "Don't worry, Sharon. I have some money in my room. I'll go get it."

Leaving Sharon at the front door, I ran into the house. My father was slouched on the sofa in the living room drinking Jim Beam whiskey. Something I did must have agitated him because by the time I raced into my room, grabbed my money, and returned, he'd jumped up from his prone position and was screaming at Sharon. "You !@#$% cheap Jew! You dirty kike. Get the hell out of here, and don't you ever come back!"

I was stunned and terrified at my father's enraged behavior. Why was he calling my friend those words? What did they even mean? Rushing over to Sharon, I pushed the money into her hand as I begged, "Daddy, no! Please don't say bad things to my friend."

Sharon left with an angry glare in my direction. I have no idea if she actually caught the bus or what happened after that. Slumping back down on the couch with his whiskey, my father ordered me to go to my room. "And don't come out!"

In tears, I obeyed. I learned later that *kike* was a demeaning ethnic slur directed at people of Jewish heritage. I didn't even know what a Jew was or how that was any different from my own ethnicity, which I'd been told was Swedish. Certainly, I saw no difference between my Jewish friend and myself. She was just another little girl like me. I felt horrified and disgusted that my father could behave so atrociously to my friend.

The next day at school, Sharon wouldn't speak to me. I pleaded with her, but she just walked away, and we never spoke again. This was my first real encounter with discrimination, and it was a hard lesson that took me a long time to understand. I didn't realize I was bearing the guilt of my father's actions rather than my own. So I thought I must be a terrible person if Sharon didn't want to be my friend. From that day on, I became fearful of making new friends. I never trusted my father again, and I never, never brought friends home.

I couldn't trust my mother either. I'm sure it isn't that unusual for parents to have a preconception of what they want their children to be. What they think their children *should* be. I in turned longed to be loved, nurtured, and free to be who I was.

That's where much of the difficulty with my mother started. She wanted a feminine little girl. What she got was a tree-climbing tomboy. I didn't want to wear pretty dresses, put my hair in curlers, or stay inside reading and playing house. I wanted to wear jeans, put my hair in a ponytail, run and play in the rain, stomp my feet in mudpuddles, and be free.

My mother often told the story of how at a very young age I would rebelliously stand my ground, hands planted firmly on my hips, look her straight in the eye, and insist, "No, I can do it my own self!"

I in turn remember vividly the disappointment on my mother's face every time I didn't measure up to what she wanted me to be. I was a resistant child with a tenacity that challenged her very motherhood.

Who then could I trust? Mean boys who shoved me down? My friend's husband who tried to molest me? A drunken father who yelled abuse at my friends? A mother who couldn't love me for who I was but only wanted to make me something I wasn't?

All these painful experiences were like arrows being shot into my childish heart. Instead of understanding that these circumstances were caused by other people who should have been protecting me, I viewed myself as the cause of trouble. My self-worth had been decimated. I told myself that I was unlovable, stupid, ugly. These lies burrowed deep within me, leading to destructive habits.

The groundwork was set. This child was growing up rebellious, angry, unable to trust anyone, self-reliant, and alone.

CHAPTER FOUR

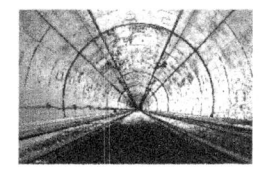

DESPAIR

What comes out of a family like ours? Well, for one thing, all of my siblings and I learned at a very early age how to survive, how to manipulate to get what we needed, and how to be strong because there just wasn't anyone to lean on. For most of my life, I continued to be like that defiant, strong-willed little girl rebelliously standing her ground and saying no to any suggestion that I become what I didn't want to be.

My memories of growing up were also of poverty, whether that was actually the case or reflected how my parents chose to live. While both my parents worked, women weren't paid well in those decades even with a pharmacy degree, and my father's government job wasn't a high-salaried position either. I don't remember my mother ever taking me shopping, and we kids fought for every penny given to us by our father.

I was only thirteen years old when I got my first summer job as a maid at one of the mountain lodges in Mount Rainier National Park not far south of Tacoma. Even for that time period, I wasn't old enough to hold such a job. But my father knew someone there and lied about my age to get me the job. It was horrible. I was a young girl barely into my teens while the other summer staff were all college age or older. After a few weeks of trying to do my best, I ran away from the mountain back home.

To this point, my father's biannual relocations had all been within the Pacific Northwest, so at least it was familiar territory. Then when I was almost sixteen years old, my father was transferred to Kansas City. This move really threw me into depression, anger, and anxiety. Everything was a culture shock as though I'd moved to the moon instead of another part of my own country. The locals talked in slow, drawn-out sentences and used unfamiliar expressions like *ya'all.* Since I didn't have a southern accent, I had only to open my mouth for everyone to know I wasn't from there.

At school, I felt like an outcast in a foreign land. I became a loner, eating my lunch in a restroom stall with my feet up so no one could see my shoes and know who I was. On some days, I could hear another scared girl having her lunch in a separate stall. I wanted desperately to talk to her, but I was too afraid.

One reason I hated school was because I was constantly behind in my studies. Our family transfers every two years for my father's job made it almost impossible to get any kind of consistent education. Each school had its own way of teaching, and the books were all so different. In some places, I was required to just attend class and the teachers would pass me on to the next grade. But that left me further and further behind my classmates. Always being the outsider struggling to catch up in class and make new friends left me with no self-confidence or pride in my accomplishments.

It didn't help that my hero older brother didn't make the move to Kansas City with the rest of us. He'd continued to be the target of physical, verbal, and emotional abuse by my father to an extent that broke my heart. Over the years, he'd run away repeatedly. He told me much later that he'd lived on the street with some other homeless people. I was always frantic until he was found and brought back as he was my only security.

By high school, he was very popular with other students. He was a handsome young man and sang in talent shows with a band that was all black students except for him. He would have been seventeen when we moved to Kansas City, and I don't even know why he didn't move with us or even if he finished high school. As soon as he could do so legally, he joined the Air Force and never looked back. Maybe he completed his high school studies there.

After four years in the Air Force, my brother became a police officer in California. He must have earned a high school diploma by then as he eventually got a college degree, a master's, and a doctorate in criminal justice. Today he is a very successful criminal justice consultant, and I remain as proud of my hero as I'd been in our childhood.

But though I was happy for him that he'd escaped our miserable homelife and my father's abuse, his absence left me feeling even more isolated and friendless. I got a job as a waitress at a restaurant and worked every shift possible just to keep from having to attend any school functions like football games, dances, other activities. Working was my escape, and I worked hard. It wasn't uncommon for me to work until midnight, walk all the way home in the dark, go to bed for just a few hours, then get up early the next day for school.

The few friends I did make in high school were all guys, as I found them safer than trying to make friends with the girls. I had one horrible memory of being jumped by a gang of girls from one of the many schools I'd attended before Kansas City who seemed to have some beef with my older brother being in an otherwise all-black band. One more lesson in not trusting people and one reason I found hiding in a bathroom stall safer than trying to break into my new school's girl cliques.

One of these guy friends named Steven became my first tragic acquaintance with death. I wasn't dating him or any of the others. In fact, I'd never had a boyfriend. They were just casual friends. Steven's first love was his beautiful red sportscar. He liked to race along empty roads at night, pushing his car to the limit just to see how fast it could go. On one cold January night, he careened around a corner well above the speed limit, tires screeching on the icy pavement. The car spun out of control, flying over the embankment like an arrow searching for a target. It smashed into a tree, totaling the car and instantly killing Steven.

We were only sixteen, and I'd never faced the death of a close friend or relative. Walking into the church for Steven's funeral, I saw it packed with all the people who loved him and were now mourning this terrible tragedy. I looked down into the open casket. The person I saw lying there was my young, handsome friend and it wasn't. He looked so pale and cold with no life in him. Where had he gone? Had he just floated up to that place called heaven I'd learned about in church as a child? Was I to believe that any more than I still believed in Santa or the Tooth Fairy?

By this time, my childhood faith in God was long-gone. In a few short years, I'd changed from a trusting little girl to a teenager full of anger and rebellion. Far from wanting to be around the people and things of God or be closer to God, I'd become completely disillusioned by the harsh realities of life. I couldn't understand how a loving and good God could allow horrible things to happen to people.

That was where my questioning really started. I went from asking how God could let such injustice and unfairness happen to questioning whether God existed at all. If God was really out there, why didn't He just show Himself? Why these games of hide and seek?

In my heart of hearts, I still wanted desperately to believe in something. I researched other religions, looking for answers. I begged every person I knew of any faith, "Please help me believe."

But no matter where I turned, nobody had any answers that made sense to me. When people saw that I didn't buy into their belief, they would tell me to "just have faith." Well, I *didn't* just have faith, and I had no idea how to get it. Given the evidence all around me that love was scarce and life was cruel, why should I have faith? What had faith ever done for me?

I especially had difficulty accepting such assertions to *just have faith* from Christians of whatever denominational church background. What proof was there that God even existed other than the testimony of some people who insisted that He did? Had any of them ever actually seen God? These people used phrasing like *born again* and *saved* and *ask Jesus into your heart*. What did those words even mean? What was the point of believing in someone you couldn't see or touch or hear?

My life went on working long hours as a waitress, going to school, and hiding in the bathroom because I didn't fit in. Then one day a girl at school who had always seemed quite nice invited me to some sort of Christian youth meeting. I no longer believed in Christianity, and my experience by this point was that most faith-centered teen gatherings were made up of cliques, always leaving me the odd girl out. But I so desperately wanted to have friends that I accepted her invitation.

To my disappointment, I felt as horribly alone at this Christian youth meeting as I had at all the other ones. A lot of popular television shows, movies, and pop music at this time idealized California life. Rock and roll hits like California Girls by the Beach Boys, California Soul, California Nights, California Dreamin', California Sun, even California Earthquake all talked up sunshine, beach parties, surfing, and other things kids in Kansas City never got to experience. From the moment I walked into this meeting, I was pointed out as *the blonde surfer girl from California.*

Never mind that I was actually from Washington State and had never been surfing. I was blonde and from the west coast, so I must be from California. What a joke! The girls stared and were standoffish. The boys seemed afraid to talk to me. So as usual, I was left standing alone, embarrassed, and vowing never to go back there again.

As my questions about God went unanswered, I went from no longer believing in God's existence to becoming very bitter and angry at anyone stupid enough to buy into this God thing. As a naive child, I'd believed in something blindly, and it had given me great hope and pleasure. Now in my teen years, it felt as though all such trusting belief had been ripped out of me. I honestly tried to believe in God, but my rebellious heart pulled me away from faith into agnosticism and then full atheism.

That said, denying God's existence didn't make me feel any better. What would happen if I died someday? Would I just fall into nothingness?

Of course, as I eventually came to realize, there is no such thing as a life without complications. Young people die horrible deaths. Friends and family leave. Human beings are constantly selfish and mean to each other. Life itself can be very cruel. Bad things happen to the best and worst of people, and I had no reason to expect anything else.

But at that time, it felt as though every hope and dream I'd ever had was trampled underfoot and there was no point in even trying anymore. I needed someone, anyone, who could encourage me that there was a single good reason to keep on living. But I had no one in whom I could confide or trust to really care about me, much less love me. The one person I continued to trust and idealize, my hero big brother, was far away in the Air Force and no longer part of our family.

To numb my pain, I started on a self-destructive path where I took up drinking and pushed absolutely everything to the limit. There was no accountability to anyone, certainly not to God since I no longer believed in Him. I'd lost the faith of my childhood, and my heart had grown hardened by sin's deceitfulness.

Chapter Five

The Vow

"Come on, Laura," I yelled at my friend. "Let's go buy some beer."

In Kansas City, the legal age for drinking was eighteen. Not yet seventeen, I looked old enough to drink, so my friends coaxed me into buying Schlitz beer at the little bar down the street. Into the bar I went with all the confidence of a full-blown adult.

Walking up to the bartender, I meant to say, "give me two six packs of Schlitz." What came out instead was "give me two shit packs of six."

Everyone in the bar exploded in laughter. Humiliated, I looked around for the nearest hole into which I could duck. The bartender was practically doubled over with hilarity as he put the beer on the counter. At least he didn't question whether I was an adult or ask to see any I.D. I paid and slid sheepishly out the door. Just as my parents had done, I was now finding my escape in drinking.

That said, I continued to work very hard at my restaurant job. I saved my money until I was able to buy a car, a shiny baby-blue convertible that I loved. My school was only four blocks from our house, so Mom immediately commandeered my car for herself and told me I could walk to school. As a minor living in her home, I had no choice. Rain, sleet, snow, I walked those four blocks to school. But the injustice of her actions made me even angrier than I'd already become.

As I headed into my senior year of high school, I just assumed I would go on to college. But when I asked my father about college, he laughed at me. "Kathy, you are not college material. You'll just get married someday."

An older guy named Al Wheeler worked as a mechanic at the gas station next to the restaurant where I was a waitress. Twenty-three to my seventeen years old, he seemed very adult and worldly-wise. He was so funny and could always make me laugh.

I had longed for so many years to have someone I could confide in. Someone to love me. Someone to give me a reason for living. It was clear Al really liked me. Even though I knew he wasn't the right person for me, he was the only one who showed an interest, so I began hanging out with him. He would buy alcohol for the two of us, and after I got off work, we would take off in his car and drink. Instead of going to football games, dances, or other wholesome activities with my high school peers, drinking away the hours with this older guy became my futile escape from reality.

The truth was that my self-esteem had tumbled so far down I'd given up trying to fit in at school, and I had no interest in subjecting myself to unkindness and rejection from other students at football games or dances. Graduation day was anticlimactic. Mom attended, but my father didn't bother. Other classmates had parties planned to celebrate, but I wasn't invited. I guess my parents assumed I was as they made no plans for any kind of celebration. I ended up driving around just to kill time so they wouldn't realize I'd been left out.

At least Al was always there and more than happy to spend time with me. But reality set in quickly when I found out that I was pregnant, the result of a drunken episode. Telling my parents was horrible. My mother was furious while my father kept demanding angrily why I was so stupid. Any remaining self-esteem fell even further.

Then Mom informed me that she would make arrangements for an abortion. That roused me to push back. Just as when I was a little girl, she was making plans on my behalf without even consulting my wishes.

"No, I won't do that!" I said firmly.

But it seemed the only options I was offered were abortion or marriage. This was 1960, not a time when raising a child out of wedlock was acceptable. The thought of murdering a little helpless baby was beyond anything I could possibly imagine. My parents didn't even suggest the option of giving my child up for adoption, and I never considered it either. That left marriage to my child's father, an alcoholic mechanic I did not love.

Still, hadn't my father said marriage was the only thing I was fit for? And could marriage to Al Wheeler be any worse than my current empty life walking into school fearful, ashamed, and humiliated, hiding my feet in the bathroom stall so no one would know I was there, working hard every spare minute to avoid other teens and my own family? At least marrying Al would mean an escape from my own miserable homelife.

So the stage was set. At eighteen years old, I would marry Al Wheeler and become a mom. Al picked me up at six a.m. on a humid summer morning, and we drove to Paris, Oklahoma, which permitted same-day marriages. I determined to be the best wife and mother I could be. But that too was an escape from reality as I was just a kid myself. A kid who'd never had a chance to grow up.

We rented a small house close to my parents. I worked as a title clerk at an automobile dealership while Al continued his mechanic job. A few months later, I gave birth to a beautiful baby boy, whom we named Christopher. Twenty-one months later, his brother Mark came along. My mother helped with childcare so I could keep working.

By now, my hopes of an escape from my previous unhappy, empty life had evaporated. Despite two incomes, we had no money. This was because Al spent much of what he made on alcohol. I shouldn't have been so surprised considering alcohol was the common bond around which our relationship had developed just as had been the case with my parents.

Al routinely came home drunk. He also hid alcohol all over the house, in the dog food bag, garbage can, everywhere. When he took out the garbage or fed the dog, he would unearth his hidden stash and drink. He snored loudly and always smelled of stale beer.

Despite this, Christopher and Mark adored their father. They found him as funny as I'd once found him. He spent hours on the floor with them, wrestling, tickling, and laughing. They couldn't see any of the bad in him.

But I did. One day we were visiting a relative's house. Al was passed out cold from drinking all day. Angry and disappointed, I tried to shake him awake. "Al, wake up! It's time to go home. The boys are tired, and so am I."

He didn't move, so I leaned over to shake him a bit harder. "Al, wake up!"

He came out of his stupor with his fist doubled up, slamming it into my mouth. The blow pushed my teeth into my lip, leaving me bleeding profusely. Another time, he took a baseball bat to me when I refused to pick up his cigarettes.

Life was so depressing I wanted to die. I had vivid nightmares that kept me terrified even after I was awake. I would look down at my hand and see it disengaging from my arm. Or I'd be running across a field when I suddenly started falling into a huge pit filled with an enormous blazing furnace, above which I was being dangled over the edge by my feet as my mother's stepfather had once done to me on a ship while in a drunken rage. Other times, an evil skeleton in a black cape and riding a black horse chased me with a sword.

Please, let me sleep without the horrible nightmares! I cried out internally. *Please, can someone explain the rage in me?*

But I received no answer. My doctor told me I was having a nervous breakdown and that I needed to get out of my marriage because it was literally destroying me. I would have loved to take his advice, but how? At just twenty-one years old, I was trapped in a miserable marriage with two little babies and an abusive drunk who couldn't make a living for his family. I couldn't see any alternative except suicide. I thought about this a lot. The only thing that kept me from acting was not knowing what would happen to my beautiful, precious sons. How could I risk leaving them to be raised by a drunken, abusive man like Al Wheeler?

With each passing day, I grew more angry and desperate as I recognized that once again I had only myself to lean on. But this time, I had two tiny innocent babies also depending on me. I tried my best to be a good mother to my sons, but when they screamed non-stop, I would sometimes just space out. Other times I would cower on the floor of the bathroom, not daring to approach my sons for fear I might do them harm. My own overwhelming stress was passed on to the boys, and together we cried our way through each day.

I was drowning in despair, and it seemed no one cared about us. Not family. Not God. No one. Then came a beautiful summer night. It was the kind of night where the stars are so bright it feels you could reach out and touch them.

Staring out the front window of our house, I raised my gaze to watch the stars glisten and twinkle. Their sheer immensity and beauty were overwhelming. I could almost feel myself leaving this life, floating up into the heavens, and becoming one with this great universe. I found myself asking how this magnificent beauty could ever have just happened by chance. Was it possible that maybe, just maybe, there really was a God Who had created all of this?

Then the loud, harsh sounds of drunken snoring brought me abruptly back down to the desperate reality in which I lived. The smell of stale beer wafted out from the bedroom, churning my stomach with disgust. Guilt flowed over me as I realized my two precious little sons were fast asleep in the next room with no idea their mother wanted to leave them behind and everything else in this life and just die.

Tears burned my eyes and ran down my cheeks. Looking up again at that spectacular night sky, I made a vow, not even sure anyone was hearing me.

God, if You really exist, I ask only one thing. I've never felt love. Give me one year of happiness, one year of knowing true love. God, if You are really there, that's all I ask. Then You can take everything I have, my life, everything, and let me die.

I turned away, convinced my words were flying through empty space. Regardless of nature's beauty, the likelihood that God wasn't there seemed more plausible than that He was. After all, how many years had I searched desperately for something to believe in only to find my heart more and more convinced that God didn't exist?

Still, even though I continued to doubt the existence of God, I reiterated my vow. If I'd done only one thing right since starting on my self-destructive, sinful path back in high school, crying out to God on that brilliant star-strewn Kansas City night was it. I had no idea the long-term impact that feeble, doubting, self-focused prayer would make in my life.

CHAPTER SIX

ESCAPE

Not long after that night, I realized my only option was to escape my abusive marriage. The rest of my family except my older brother had by now moved back to the Pacific Northwest, the region I still considered home. So one day while Al was out of the house, I packed up a few belongings and what little money I had. Then I gathered my two beautiful sons and loaded them and our scant possessions into the old Plymouth Valiant I drove. I never did get my baby-blue convertible back from my mother.

Christopher—or Chris, as we called him—was four years old now with a shock of flaxen-blonde hair, hazel eyes, and a personality that was always uplifting, funny, and wise for his age. Two-year-old Mark had the same blonde hair but strikingly beautiful green eyes and was more mischievous by nature.

As we drove away from Kansas City, Chris piped up to ask, "Mommy, where are we going?"

"We're going to Seattle where Grandma and Grandpa live," I responded.

"Is Daddy coming with us?" Chris asked anxiously.

"No Chris. Daddy can't come this time."

Those words seared through me. Waves of fear and anxiety brought tears as I faced the reality that I was driving two thousand miles, then starting a new life as a single mom completely on my own. The highway ahead of me blurred through my tears even as I kept my voice cheerful to sooth my two sons, who kept asking for their daddy. Determination banished my tears as I reminded myself of the miserable life we were escaping.

Once we arrived in Seattle, I quickly found accommodations for my sons and me in a government-subsidized housing unit that was part of a large complex of rowhouse duplexes built for low-income families and single parents. We moved in with nothing but sleeping bags, cold cereal, and hundreds of cockroaches. I called my parents for help. They lived in Federal Way, a town thirty miles south of Seattle near Tacoma.

"You made your bed, now lie in it!" sums up their general response.

My father did say that anytime we were hungry, we could come for dinner. Which wasn't particularly helpful since I didn't have gas money to get there. I would have to make it on my own. We literally ate Cheerios breakfast, lunch, and dinner.

But while I was terrified to be living alone with my little boys, no food, and no money, I was also determined to make something of my life and a better existence for my sons. I knew this life couldn't be worse than the life I'd just left. That gave me the strength and courage to forge onward.

By now I'd phoned Al to let him know where we were and why we'd left. I also made clear I was filing for divorce and full custody of our sons. I didn't anticipate any difficulty getting either as by the time I'd left Kansas City, Al had built up an extensive criminal record, including counterfeit checks and bank fraud along with extensive alcohol-related misdemeanors. Because defrauding a bank was a federal offense, he was on the FBI watchlist.

Sure enough, Al didn't contest the divorce or follow us to Seattle. In fact, during the divorce proceedings he simply disappeared, leaving no forwarding information. I found out later that the authorities in Kansas City were looking for him to arrest him, so he'd gone on the run. His disappearance signified that he paid no child support either. But I preferred to struggle on my own if that meant having him out of our lives.

I went from business to business, knocking on doors and asking for any available work. My eagerness interested one employer, an auto dealer by the name of Mr. Grant, who offered me a job. At first, this was just calling a list of customers to thank them for choosing his dealership and let them know how much their business meant to him as the owner.

I should note here that back in the 1960s and 70s, the auto industry had a terrible reputation. Car salesmen were paid by commission only, which meant losing a sale could mean losing that month's house payment. So many of them were hard-selling characters who would do just about anything to sell a car—and I mean anything!

I'd been fascinated by the auto industry since I was a small child because it was one of the rare parts of his life in which my father let me participate. He purchased a new car every two years, and he would take me with him to the dealerships, letting me smell the new cars and touch their beautiful, shiny paint. He found bargaining with auto dealers to be the highest form of mental achievement and would train for his bargaining like some Olympic athlete, always striving to get the best deal in history.

In truth, people had reason to be leery of car salesmen. But car buyers like my father could be just as avaricious, trying to take advantage of the sellers to get the greatest deal ever. So once I began working for Mr. Grant and realized this car dealer wasn't some huge, hairy monster out to swindle the public but an honest businessman who loved his family, cared about his customers, and gave honest service, I was hooked.

As I began calling customers, I soon turned up a lot of information I became convinced could help Mr. Grant run a better business. There were two basic types of customers I was dealing with. First were customers who had just purchased a brand-new car. I would call to thank them and ask how things were going with their new purchase. The other type of customers were people who had brought their cars into the auto dealership service department for repairs. I worked from repair orders that gave me the customer's name, address, and phone number as well as the age and mileage of the car they'd brought in to be serviced.

When I called these customers, I would thank them for choosing our business and ask if they were satisfied with the service they'd received. Boy, did I get an earful! I took the information to my boss. Up until this point, Mr. Grant had no way of knowing what customers were saying or how they felt, so he was shocked at some of the reports of bad service I had received. A few days later, I heard that the service manager had been fired.

It truly was surprising the huge amount of information that could be unearthed just by calling to say thank you and asking how the customer had found their experience at our business. Mr. Grant couldn't get enough of these reports and waited eagerly each day for me to bring them into him. In the second week after I started work there, my job description was expanded to Customer Relations Manager.

Wow, from unemployed to manager in just over a week! I was enthusiastic about the value I was bringing to both the customers and the business. If I could convince our customers that Mr. Grant's dealership was honest, cared about the customers, and stood behind their product, then I knew they would become customers for life. They in turn would recommend our business to other people. What better advertising than a friend or family member vouching for the business?

I loved my job, and as a perk of working at an auto dealership, I had a brand-new car to drive. But my wages didn't increase, so life remained a constant financial struggle for me and the boys. One day, I asked Mr. Grant if I could try selling cars. I didn't realize there were no women in this field. He hesitated, then said yes.

I started the next day on the display floor eager to sell my first car and make a commission. The other sales personnel were a tight-knit bunch who had never worked with a woman, and they huddled together on the far side of the floor, staring at me. This made me feel very uncomfortable.

When it was my turn to handle the next customer, a very nice family came through the door. I greeted them warmly and within an hour had sold my first car. It was so exciting and fun, and I looked forward to being able to make enough money to support my family and live a normal life.

Then came the reality of that time period. All the other sales personnel walked off the floor, refusing to work with a woman. This was the way it was in the 1960s. Women were supposed to stay home and take care of the house and family. Working women were accused of taking away money from the men who were supposed to support those families. Divorced women were looked down on with even more disdain. That I had a family to support too didn't matter.

Furious, I went to Mr. Grant. He sympathized with my frustration but couldn't keep his business open without experienced sales personnel. I returned to my desk. It seemed making phone calls was the best I'd be allowed to do.

But as I continued calling customers who brought their cars to the service department, I noticed many of those cars had very high mileage. That had to be costing customers a lot of money in repairs. When I made follow-up calls to these customers, I began asking if they'd considered buying a newer car and getting rid of all those repair bills.

I found prospect after prospect of people who wanted to buy a newer car. I would then turn those leads over to the salesmen, who sold them new cars. Which of course helped them to support their families as they'd denied me the opportunity to better support mine. But my purpose in doing this was to build customer satisfaction for Mr. Grant's business whether or not the sales benefited me.

Telemarketing wasn't even popularized until the 1980s. There were no J.D. Power Dealer of Excellence awards or other programs that focused on recognizing and rewarding customer satisfaction. So what I was doing at Mr. Grant's dealership in the 1960s was a forerunner of an entire new industry that hadn't even been conceived of yet. To the best of my knowledge, the system I started there was the first workplace customer satisfaction program in the United States and maybe even that entire region of the planet.

On a chilly, rainy January day, I scurried into the dealership shivering from the cold. I didn't have a warm coat because I just couldn't afford one. The salesmen had noticed my lack of a warm coat and wanted to show appreciation for the many sales leads I'd sent them, so they'd taken up a collection. As I entered, they all gathered together and approached me. "Kathy, we took up this collection, and we want you to go buy yourself a coat."

I was so excited as I'd recently seen a modestly priced Navy-style coat in a store window just down the street. It had brass buttons and beautiful red satin lining. I'd fallen in love with that coat and immediately headed down the street to make the purchase. It was such a good deal I even had a couple dollars left over from their collection.

I walked back into the dealership. The salesmen were still standing around as no customers had arrived. As I walked past, one of the salesmen named Bob grabbed me by the collar of my new coat so tightly I almost choked.

"Hey, we didn't mean for you to go buy an expensive coat like this!" he sneered. "My wife would look great in this coat."

I was so shocked I started to tremble, but I managed to respond coolly. "It wasn't that expensive. If you want, I'll take it back, and you can go down there and buy it for her."

Despite my calm words, the pain and anger welling up inside of me was visible enough that the other salesmen immediately told Bob to back off and leave me alone. I walked away, feeling ashamed and embarrassed.

Still, even with such unpleasant incidents, I was proud of what I was accomplishing in this male-dominated profession. Customer satisfaction had never really been addressed before the 1960s, so I was making up my job as I went along. I wrote job descriptions and held manager meetings. What I discovered was how to earn people's trust. In the auto industry, we're talking some very hard-core elements, so building trust in a car dealership was a challenge. There are a few individuals who take credit for initiating the wave of customer satisfaction with surveys and such in the United States. But none of them were doing such work in the 1960s.

In the process, I gained a lot of self-confidence. I learned to stand up for myself. To speak back to injustice. To crawl into the trenches and build something beautiful out of mud.

And Mr. Grant and his wife loved me. They saw me as a major asset to their business. I was keeping their service department honest and upright and causing sales to go through the roof. I was teaching salesmen how to approach people in an honest, forthright way. I sat on arbitration boards to help solve disputes. It seems that in my years of hard-scrabble living, I'd developed a keen ability to think on the run and bluff my way into a top management position.

Chapter Seven

Will You Be My Daddy?

"Chris, would you bring me that pile of whites?" I called to my older son as I deposited a load of dirty clothing into a laundromat washing machine. "Mark, quit running out the door."

I was exhausted from a long day at the auto dealership, but the duties of a single mom were not yet done. Laundry. Baths. Grocery shopping. Would it never end?

I settled my sons down to eat the fast-food order that was our dinner while we waited for our laundry. A man was folding his clothes nearby. Suddenly, Chris walked over to him and asked, "Mister, will you be my daddy?"

I stood there in shock, not knowing what to say. Thankfully, the man just looked at me and smiled, paying no attention to this young boy who was trying to fill a hole in his little heart. I knew my sons still missed Al as they often asked the question that seared through me like a sword, plunging deep into my heart. "Mommy, where is Daddy?"

How could I tell them that their daddy was in jail again or too drunk to talk to them? Al did call occasionally, wanting to talk to the boys, always when he was extremely drunk. But that usually ended up in a screaming match over his alcohol addiction and criminal doings. Not once did he send any financial support for his sons, Christmas gifts, birthday gifts, nothing to indicate he really cared about the boys. They were just a means to get to me.

Because Al refused to pay child support and my own salary remained very low, I was unable to escape the government housing and poverty we were forced to live in. Somehow, the boys and I made the best of things. We became geniuses at finding gems of second-hand clothing, dishes, and other household needs at the local Good Will. A little gas stove heated our housing unit. We would pull our sleeping bags up close and pretend it was a bonfire and that we were camping.

I also found a nice older woman to watch the boys so I could immerse myself into work. I loved those little boys more than my life and suffered waves of guilt over leaving them at *Grandma Dorsey's Childcare*, as I affectionately termed her. Sometimes I worked so late that she would feed them dinner, which at least gave them a decent meal. I was so thankful for her as I would not have been able to excel at my job without her help.

Then when all seemed to be finally going well, something else horrible happened. I made a stupid, stupid mistake, and to this day I am ashamed of my choices. Al had disappeared during the divorce proceedings, leaving no forwarding information. But not long after I'd started my job with Mr. Grant, he arrived in Seattle. Tracking down my address, he came to our government housing unit and demanded to see the boys. I was so scared, lonely, and confused, and my sons wanted so desperately to see their daddy that I let him move in with us. Once again, I found myself pregnant.

Let me make clear that I'm against abortion in every way. For many years, I've been involved with *Mamma's House*, a Palm Springs, CA, ministry to unwed young mothers that helps them have their babies, finish their education, find jobs and housing, and build a new life for themselves.

But at this time, I had no belief in God or the sanctity of human life from the moment of conception. I'd pushed back against my mother when she'd wanted me to have an abortion instead marrying Al and having my sons Chris and Mark. But it didn't take long for Al's renewed drunken, abusive behavior to remind me why I'd fled from him to Seattle. I had no intention of rekindling our relationship, and I felt I just couldn't have another child with such a horrible, horrible man.

In November 1970, Washington became the first state to legalize early pregnancy abortions through a vote of the people. But in the mid-1960s, abortion was still illegal, and there was no such thing as *safe* medical facilities for an abortion. I found the name of a man in eastern Washington State who performed abortions, and Al drove me there.

The man carried out the abortion in an old barn. I don't know if he was a doctor or had been one. But the sanitary conditions were disgusting and the setup very primitive. There was no anesthetic, so I was wide-awake and could feel everything. The barn was remote enough from any other residences that no one could hear my screams. It was horrible!

When he'd finished, the man commented, "Isn't this too bad! It's a healthy baby boy!"

Those words will go with me to my grave. Thankfully, despite the unhygienic conditions and rough handling, I survived. Later when I married Don, there was nothing I wanted more than to have his child, but I wondered how much damage I'd done to myself.

Al soon disappeared again, for which I was thankful. I've asked God to forgive me over and over for that abortion. I know He has, and He eventually even blessed Don and me with our son Dusty. But I doubt I will ever completely forgive myself this side of heaven. All part of my visit to hell in my near-death experience on that awful day. I truly am a sinner redeemed!

I've never shared this story before with even my closest friends and family. But though I am still ashamed at my choices then, I feel it is important to share now just because so many women today are taught that abortion is no big deal, that their own convenience is all that matters, and that they won't regret killing their child in the womb.

I am here to testify that this isn't true, and the stain of taking this child's life will haunt me till I die. An unborn child is a beautiful person created by God from the moment of conception and deserves the opportunity to live. So if you are considering abortion or know someone who is, please consider going instead to one of the countless organizations that help pregnant women and give this baby a chance at life. You won't regret it.

Chapter Eight

Torn Apart

My job responsibilities continued to expand. I'd been in Seattle for about a year when Mr. Grant authorized hiring an assistant for me. While I was interviewing possible candidates, a petite blonde woman with a markedly British accent walked into my office.

"Here, take my wrap," she ordered, handing me her coat.

I stared at her, a bit perplexed at her audacity. Didn't she realize I was her potential boss? But I liked her spunk, and by the end of the interview I'd hired her.

Originally from the Isle of Man in the Irish Sea between Britain and Ireland, Brenda had married an American man from Seattle named Lanny, which was how she'd ended up in the United States. She had no more experience working in an auto dealership than I'd had when I started. But she had a very take-charge personality and quickly grew into the job I'd created for her. We also became good friends.

With my long working hours and two preschool children, I'd had no time for friends to this point. But Brenda and her husband

Lanny changed that. During the summer months, they left their suburban home for an RV parked in a private campground on the shore of a beautiful lake. They had a very comfortable lifestyle set up there, and when they weren't working, they spent morning till dark water-skiing, swimming, and enjoying the warm summer days.

Brenda and Lanny had a son about the age of Chris, and they insisted the boys and I spend the summer at the lake with them. I took them up on their offer. Living in a tent with two small boys was crowded but so much fun compared to our government housing. My sons were elated with so many places to run and play. We all pitched in to watch the boys and prepare meals. On workdays, Brenda and I would drive in to the dealership while the boys stayed with Lanny at the lake. After work, we'd take their boat out on the lake and ski until dark. Sometimes on clear nights, we'd ski after dark in the moonlight.

Finally, my life seemed to be going the right direction. I absolutely loved living by the water. I'd learned to water ski in high school on trips to Lake of the Ozarks, a large water reservoir in Missouri about three hours' drive from Kansas City. Some guys from a professional water ski show I met there taught me maneuvers not many could do. At my young, carefree age, I would just go for it, not even thinking of the potential risk.

Then at just eighteen, I was married and became a mother. How I'd missed being on the water during those years of married life in Kansas City. To my surprise, I found that my skiing ability came right back once I got out on the lake. I would hit the water with Brenda for hours while Lanny watched the boys. We were both exceptional skiers and would always draw a crowd along the shore to watch us do tricks in, out, and under the tow ropes. I loved this life. I couldn't have been happier.

One day out on the lake with a single ski, I pulled hard and went into a turn with my shoulder, almost touching the water. Coming into the shore with superb timing, I stepped off my ski onto the beach without a single slip. The day was overcast and a bit chilly, so I scurried around making coffee on the small camp stove I had set up outside our tent.

I had finished my coffee and was about to head back to the lake when I heard an all-too-familiar voice. "Hello, Kathy."

My blood turned to ice. Slowly, I turned around to find Al standing behind me. I could tell he was drunk just from the smell, which filled my nostrils like the putrid stench of rotting garbage.

"What are you doing here?" I demanded. "How did you find me?"

"I want to see my sons," he slurred with a condescending grin. "You can't keep me from seeing them."

"They aren't your sons anymore!" I responded defiantly. "I have full custody. You've been gone for more than a year without so much as sending a birthday card or Christmas present. You have no right to just walk back into their lives and hurt them again. Go away! Get out of here!"

Then I heard my six-year-old son Chris squeal with joyous excitement. "Daddy, daddy, daddy!"

I watched in horrified dismay as Chris ran into Al's arms. Mark quickly followed. This was more than I could bear. Just as in the past, my first reaction was to run. I wasn't worried Al hurt the boys or even try to take them since he had no interest in taking responsibility for two small children. And I knew how upset my sons would be if I didn't let them spend some time with their daddy now that he was here. But neither did I want to stay there and see my ex-husband slobbering drunkenly over my sons or witness their delight at his visit. It would just hurt my sons to tell them what a horrible monster he was.

Since I could trust Lanny to keep an eye on the boys, I pulled on my ski vest and told Brenda, "Take me out, please."

We headed out onto the lake, Brenda driving the boat and me pulling out all my most difficult maneuvers on my ski. Angry and frustrated, I kept signaling Brenda to go faster and faster. The sun wasn't shining that day, and the lake looked dark and foreboding. I pulled harder and harder on the rope, diving into turns and skimming over the water faster than I'd ever gone before.

Confusion intermixed with rage surged through me as I tried to think how I should handle this confrontation with my ex-husband. I knew he had warrants out for his arrest, both for past criminal behavior and well over a year of unpaid child support. All I had to do was call the police and he'd be gone again. But that too would hurt my sons horribly. At that moment, there was no one in the world I hated more than Al Wheeler for putting me in this situation.

Pulling with all my strength, I started into a steep turn. The speed of the boat must have been forty miles an hour, and I was going twice that fast in a 360-degree turn when I felt myself slip. Crashing into the dark, murky lake was like slamming into a brick wall. I twisted and turned through the water like a stray bullet. In my panicked state, I had no sense of direction. Was I going up or down deeper?

As the water grew darker and darker, I realized I must be spiraling deeper than I'd ever gone before. The ski hadn't popped off my foot at impact as it should have, and I knew all the twisting and turning would be catastrophic for my body.

Just relax! The vest will bring you up. It seemed to take forever, and my lungs were burning by the time my head broke the surface. Gasping for air, I looked around frantically for the tow boat. It seemed so far away. Wasn't Brenda watching?

The boat turned, and a few moments later, Brenda drew up beside me. She cheerfully pointed out the obvious. "That was quite a tumble you took."

I had climbed into the boat countless times that summer, but this time I could barely pull myself high enough out of the water to climb in. Falling to the floor of the boat, I curled into a ball, holding my leg. "I think I'm hurt!"

"Hey, let's get back to shore, and you can walk it off," Brenda responded.

When we reached the lakeshore, I tried to put weight on my leg, but I immediately collapsed to the ground. Lanny and Brenda helped me to the tent and out of my wet clothes. Bewildered and in shock, I huddled down into my bed, shaking from the pain. Al was still visiting with the boys but soon left.

By the next morning, my leg had swollen to twice its normal size. Brenda rushed me to the hospital. I'd had little contact with my parents since moving to Seattle. Now I saw no alternative but to call them. Especially with Al back in town as I didn't want him around my sons while I was incapacitated.

My parents weren't happy at the call, but they took the boys. From the emergency ward, I was rushed into surgery. When I came out of the anesthetic, the surgeon informed me, "You have had a very serious accident, young lady. You almost lost your leg. We did the best we could with what was left."

I had literally twisted my leg apart at the knee, separating and tearing all the ligaments, tendons, everything. The only thing still holding my leg on my body was the skin that surrounded it. The doctors had been unable to reconnect or even find the main ligament that ran through the middle of my knee.

The days that followed were grueling and painful. The hospital was in the middle of a nurses' strike. Due to being left unattended for long periods of time, I developed blood clots, swelling, and infection around my heart. Pneumonia set in, and I came close to dying. All I could think about were my little boys and who was going to care for them. In your early twenties, facing a disability isn't something you really think about. I was strong and healthy, so I assumed I'd be fine.

Once I left the hospital, my parents took me in along with my two sons. This was at best an awkward situation since I'd never had a good relationship with either parent. Both my younger siblings still lived at home as well, making for extremely crowded living conditions. I was grateful for my parents' help, but all I wanted was my little government housing unit, our gas stove, and to be alone again.

My recovery was long and painful, and my leg would never be the same. But I was finally able to move back into our housing unit. I looked forward to returning to work and once again starting to build a life for the boys and myself.

But when my sons and I entered our unit, I found it stripped of anything that had monetary value. I learned that Al had the audacity to move into my home while I was rehabbing. Though he was gone by the time I got there, he'd taken our food, anything that could be sold or pawned, even a jar of coins I'd been collecting to buy shoes for Mark since his shoes had holes in the toes.

The one bit of good news was that Al had once again disappeared. The FBI had come looking for him, whether for his past crimes or new ones. They even brought me to their Seattle headquarters for questioning. I had nothing I could tell them they didn't already know. I was just thankful there was never a suggestion that I'd taken any part in his criminal behavior.

They also asked me to file nonpayment of child support charges against Al as they considered him a serious menace to society and wanted to do everything possible to keep him in prison if they caught him. I hadn't pushed for such charges because I didn't want any further contact with him. But the district attorney questioning me pointed out that the money wasn't mine. It belonged to the boys, and as such it was my duty to enable the state to collect it through prosecution.

I'd already determined I'd turn Al into the police if he ever approached us again. In the end, it didn't matter as I never saw him again after that horrible day at the lake. He died a few years later just as he'd lived from the effects of alcohol poison. Life went on for the boys and me. Sadly, Chris continued to search for a *new daddy*.

My assistant Brenda had kept things going at work while I healed from my accident. Mr. Grant was so happy to have me back, and I was so grateful for this opportunity. The company had continued to pay me during my rehabilitation, which was also a rarity in the 1960s, especially for a female employee. No one had ever shown me this much respect, and it really boosted my self-confidence.

I'd been a single mom by now for over two years. I'd come to the realization that not many decent men would consider dating a divorced woman with two small children. Which was fine because another romantic relationship was the last thing on my mind. My sons and my job were my life. I would consider dinner dates since this was a good way to fill my purse with bread rolls or anything else I could take home in a *doggie bag*, as it was termed then. That would be dinner the next night.

CHAPTER NINE

TRUE LOVE FOUND

As I settled back into my job, I was grateful for the help Brenda provided. Walking remained difficult for me, and I'm sure the way I drove was illegal with my bad leg and foot resting on the gas and my other foot on the brake. I didn't really have any choice if I was to keep my job and care for my sons.

Since Brenda was always there for me at the office, she decided it was time to handle my social life as well. Early one morning about three months after the accident, the phone woke me from a sound sleep. Glancing at the clock, I saw that it was only six a.m. on a Saturday, which was my day off. Who could be calling me this early?

When I picked up the phone, it was Brenda. In a very excited voice, she began telling me about some extremely handsome man who was just the person I was going to marry.

"Brenda, it's six in the morning!" I responded with exasperation. "And I'm not going to get married again, never, never, never!"

Brenda carried on as if I hadn't spoken a word. "I told him you are a beautiful green-eyed blonde and that he is going to marry you."

I couldn't believe what she was saying. When I realized my assistant was simply not going to take no for an answer, I hung up the phone so hard it dropped from the table onto my toe. Arghhh!

The answer is NO! I informed Brenda mentally. *Married again? That would be the day!*

As I snuggled back under my covers, my heart ached just remembering what a terrible experience my marriage had been. Come to think of it, no one I knew except maybe Brenda and Lanny had a really good marriage. *No, just leave me alone! And darn it, my toe hurts!*

The phone rang again. Should I answer it? I wasn't ready to deal with another sales pitch from my assistant.

In the end, I did answer it. To my amazement, the voice on the other end wasn't Brenda but the gentlest, most calming male voice I'd ever heard. The man explained that his name was Don and he was an acquaintance of Brenda. I'm not really sure what he said after that. Just listening to his voice was comforting. He asked if I'd like to go skeet shooting with him the following evening.

I wasn't sure what a skeet was, and I really didn't want to shoot one. But the gentle male voice on the line was so appealing I blurted out, "Sure!"

As luck would have it, there was a snowstorm the next evening, saving the skeet and myself (I eventually found out that *skeet*, like *clay pigeon*, simply references tossing clay targets into the air and trying to shoot them so no actual bloodshed involved!). Instead, Don and I met up to have dinner at a restaurant. My critical eye found him very appealing in appearance at almost six feet tall with thick, dark hair and the bluest eyes I'd ever seen.

I learned that he'd spent two years of active duty in the Naval Reserves and had been in Vietnam. He was currently working as a real estate salesman. Like me, he was twenty-five years old, and he too was divorced. We both loved sports and outdoor activities. The more we talked, the more we discovered we had in common, especially the fact that neither of us wanted to get married again. Conversation was so easy with him, and he made me laugh.

For the next twenty-seven days, Don and I saw each other every evening. He seemed to enjoy coming to our cozy little unit in the government housing complex. I had purchased inexpensive furniture, and the atmosphere in our home was warm, cozy, and fun. Don also took pleasure in playing with Chris and Mark, wrestling with them on the floor, throwing them into the air.

He made them laugh too, and I felt a joy I'd never really felt in my entire life. It seemed as though Don and I had been together forever. My mother had told me that when the perfect someone for you comes along, you will know. I'd always thought her statement rather ironic considering how contentious my parents' marriage had been. But I couldn't imagine how Don could be more perfect.

On the twenty-eighth day, Don called me at work and invited me out again for that evening. Tired and busy, I suggested we take a break for one night. But Don was persistent. "Just meet me for one hour."

Hmmm, I guess I can manage one hour. That's not much. Little did I know how that single hour would change my life forever.

I met Don at a small restaurant near the real estate office where he worked. As I sat across the table looking at this handsome, gentle, loving person with dark hair and crystal-blue eyes, fear washed over me like a black plague. I also felt a strange emotion I'd never felt before. I didn't recognize what it was, but it frightened me. Could he see my heart pounding and my face turning red?

As I kept looking at Don, I suddenly realized that the strange emotion I was feeling was true love in my heart for this man. Love beyond anything I'd ever experienced except perhaps for my sons.

Don was talking away, but I didn't really hear anything he said. Everything was a blur. All I could think about was what I should do now. Because nothing ever came easily to me, I'd always fought for what I wanted and knew how to manipulate people to get it. I'd never learned how to just allow circumstances to unfold naturally. I was convinced a person needs to make things happen. Being with Don was everything to me, but I felt unworthy because he was so perfect and I was— well, I was just me!

A loud, obnoxious voice brought me back to reality. One of Don's coworkers named Bill stood looming over the table where we sat. He was very drunk, his hair disheveled and his eyes glazed over from alcohol. Leaning his large frame over the table, he got right in Don's face, wagging his finger and slurring his words. "You know what? You two belong together. What would it take for you to marry this girl?"

What did he just say? Bill's words made my heart run wild. Then Don shocked me even more as he responded, "You know what, Bill, if I had two hundred dollars, we'd leave tonight and get married."

Had Don really just said that? I sat frozen, holding my breath to see what would happen next. It was like being suspended on a rollercoaster, out of control, screaming, the excitement and adrenaline all coming together at the same moment. But I couldn't scream. Can you imagine a fairytale coming true? It was happening!

In 1968, two hundred dollars was a lot of money, equivalent in purchasing power to about two thousand dollars today. So I was stunned when Bill pulled out his checkbook and wrote a check for two hundred dollars. Don looked at me with a smile. "Well, let's go."

So off we went to Reno, Nevada, where you could get married with no waiting period. On February 9, 1968, just twenty-eight days after meeting each other, Don and I were married in the county courthouse, by Justice of the Peace William R. Beemer. We were so much in love.

When we got back, the boys and I moved into Don's house. What a difference from our cockroach-infested government housing unit! As each day dawned, it seemed like there was one wonderful surprise after another, like discovering boxes of crystal glassware and fine china Don had purchased while in the Navy and never bothered to use.

It felt as though everything in my life had finally come together without any effort from me. I hadn't done anything to cause this. I hadn't manipulated or fought. It just happened. Don was the most handsome man I had ever known. He really loved me, and I cherished him. Chris and Mark now had a real home with a mom and dad.

But however much in love, Don and I didn't really know anything about each other. How could we after just twenty-eight days acquaintance? I knew Don had been married barely out of high school to a classmate from an upper-class family. Their marriage lasted only a year before he discovered she was having an affair with her much-older boss. So I'd actually caught him on the rebound. I'm sure as the years passed that she must have regretted losing a wonderful, handsome husband like Don. But I wasn't about to let her have him back!

Don's friends and family didn't know how to take his marriage to a twenty-five-year-old sandy-blonde divorcee with two little boys. This might seem a double standard considering Don was also divorced. But in that era, divorced women were looked down on as cheap outcasts, especially those with children. I was certainly not the type of woman they'd assumed Don would end up with. It was some time before they accepted me, which caused my feelings of inadequacy and insecurity to flare up.

Chris and Mark, who were now six and four years old, weren't so sure either how to take their new daddy. They would hide away in the new bedroom they shared, talking and giggling. But for me, life had taken on a new purpose, and that purpose was one hundred percent Don. I had found true love!

CHAPTER TEN

REMEMBERING THE VOW

One evening while making meatloaf for dinner, I neglected to remove the thin layer of waxed paper dividing the hamburger sections in their cardboard container. I ended up kneading the paper right into the meatloaf. Without saying a word about my mistake, Don carefully spit out little white balls of paper and put them on his plate, then kept eating the meatloaf. That's just how he was. I had never really cooked before, but he accepted that.

Our life together was perfect. When we went for walks and he put his arm around my shoulder, I was constantly amazed how I just seemed to fit. I loved his strong hands. They protected me, those hands. Then one night at a party, I heard for the first time what happened when Don's hands touched a piano. I didn't even know he played the piano. The music was beautifully intense and perfect just like Don.

Maybe I should have been suspicious because nothing could truly be that flawless. But I was too busy with my newfound life. I treasured it with all my heart. We were the couple in the movies that always had happy endings.

Don's job as a real estate salesman working on commission somewhat frightened me. I wanted the security of a paycheck coming in every month. That said, he had accomplished wonders for just being twenty-five years old. He'd purchased his own house. He drove a nice car. He seemed to be making enough money. Beyond that, he had all the self-confidence a man could have, and that made me feel safe.

Don also played with my sons as if they were his own. But he'd never experienced a loving father relationship himself, so a lot was missing. Don's father was a Navy commander and Pearl Harbor survivor. Very smart and successful, he was as strikingly handsome as Don and had been married three times. He was never really involved with the various children he had in his three marriages. Don and two siblings were the fruit of his second marriage.

Chris and Mark were anxious little boys who needed security and desperately longed for a loving father figure to replace the daddy they'd lost. But Don had been conditioned by his father that being tough and strong was paramount. So my sons' teddy bears went in the fireplace, and the discipline started. Meanwhile, I was so caught up in my exciting new life that my own time with my sons wasn't the same. My focus was completely on my new husband, not on these little boys.

Then came our first anniversary. Don and I made plans to go out and celebrate our love for each other. I was still amazed that this wonderful, even-tempered man who had never so much as raised his voice to me was my husband. I walked over to the glass doors leading to our backyard and looked out at the beautiful flowers that bloomed even in February, thanks to Seattle's temperate climate. A sudden feeling of dread swept over me as I remembered the night back in Kansas City when I'd made my vow to a God I still wasn't sure existed.

God, if You really exist, I ask only one thing. I've never felt love. Give me one year of happiness, one year of knowing true love. God, if You are really there, that's all I ask. Then You can take everything I have, my life, everything, and let me die.

Just as I'd asked in my vow, it had been exactly one year to the very day since Don and I were married, and that year had indeed been one of complete happiness and knowing true love. As I recalled standing at the front window looking up at the stars that night back in Kansas City, I thought with a shudder of my own pledge that if God gave me that perfect year, He could then take everything I had, including my life, my sons, my true love.

I pushed away that horrible thought with all my strength. My reasoning was simple. If I refused to acknowledge the possibility that God existed, then I needn't worry that God would rain down devastation to fulfil the vow I'd made. I would just continue relying on myself.

But that day did turn out to be the end of my perfect new life. Not long before our first anniversary, Don had gone into partnership with a friend to buy a tavern with the goal of turning it into a sports bar. Neither of us knew anything about the tavern business or running any type of business, for that matter. But Don was excited at the opportunity to be his own boss and no longer depend on hit-and-miss real estate commissions.

My heart was fearful of this new adventure, in part because the very thought of being around alcohol was an unpleasant reminder of my life with Al Wheeler. But I trusted Don and his partner. I also remembered vividly how bitter my father had become when he wasn't able to pursue his dream of opening a restaurant and becoming his own boss. I didn't want to see that in my own marriage, so I supported Don's decision.

That evening, we had a wonderful first anniversary dinner. On the way home, Don suggested, "Let's stop by and see how the business is going."

"No!" my heart screamed. In the 1960s, taverns were an escape for men, especially those catering to the sports crowd. Women didn't hang out in that environment unless they were trying to pick up men, and these were usually lower-class, disreputable women, not respectable married career women such as I considered myself to be. All I wanted was to go home and enjoy a romantic anniversary evening with my husband.

But I could see how important this was to Don, so I said, "All right."

The moment we walked into the tavern, its patrons crowded around Don to congratulate him on being the new owner. One of the barmaids, Charlene, came over and gave Don a big hug and kiss on the cheek. I retreated to a back corner booth, growing more and more impatient as Don worked the crowd. While I was happy that Don was popular with his customers, it really bothered me to see this barmaid unmistakably striving to get his attention.

As time passed, I grew more and more angry with Don for leaving me there by myself. I was also embarrassed and upset that our wonderful evening had ended this way. Had he forgotten we were supposed to be on our anniversary date?

Then I noticed the barmaid Charlene flicking her long hair towards Don. As he came closer, she lifted her long hair, and he bent over her neck. He seemed to be fixing a necklace for her. That did it. I jumped up and flew out the door, leaving my coat, purse, and Don behind. A chill February wind blew right through me as I started running down the street.

I was crying hysterically, not even knowing or caring where I was headed. What had I been thinking this past year of happiness? I should have known I wasn't good enough to keep Don's love. As with so many other times in my life, all I could think of was to run, run, run as fast as I could. Maybe then the terrible pain in my soul would go away.

What a mess I was! It had started to rain, and my wet hair was plastered down and blowing across my face. Just then, a car pulled up next to me. A man's voice asked, "Lady, do you need some help? Would you like a ride?"

"Sure!" I responded. Without a moment's hesitation, I hopped into the car with a total stranger. The man didn't say a word. He just drove and drove while I played over and over in my mind what had just happened. When I was completely exhausted, he asked, "Would you like to go home now?"

"Yes, please," I said, and the man drove me home. He was so kind and understanding that I have to wonder if maybe he was an actual angel God had sent to watch over me as the Bible describes (Hebrews 13:2; Psalm 91:11). Either way, I know God sent him, and I was so blessed to have him come to my aid. He pulled up to the curb outside our house, and I jumped out of the car. As I walked up the driveway, I saw Don standing in the front door, looking angry and frustrated. I brushed past him without a word.

After that night, things changed in our perfect marriage. The arguments came out of nowhere. My life was filled with so many insecurities, and they caused me to demand things from Don he couldn't possibly give. I was looking to him to fill the void that was inside of me and needed constant reassurance that I was loved. The truth was that neither Don nor any other person could heal my self-doubt or make me happy all the time. I had so many layers of pain that had built up since childhood.

The more I pushed towards him, the more Don backed off. The more he backed off, the more unstable I became and the more I pushed. This vicious circle went on and on, causing us to pick at each other verbally and translate each other's words into something the other person never intended. Instead of trying to improve my life, I turned to alcohol and cookies. This led to gaining weight. I cut my fine blonde hair shorter and shorter, not an attractive look on me. All of which left me feeling even more ugly and unloved.

It wasn't long before Don started pulling away from his overly needy wife. It was easier for me to become angry and pick a fight than to show my pain. His way of dealing with this was to just walk away and immerse himself in sports. He'd always been very athletic, and he enjoyed baseball, basketball, soccer, tennis, racquetball, golf, in fact, pretty well anything that involved some kind of ball. If someone called for Don when he wasn't home, I could usually say with honesty, "He's out chasing a ball."

Don was also a total flirt at that time. Women were always attracted to him, and he loved the attention they gave him. I wasn't capable of giving him that attention because I didn't feel worthy to walk alongside him. He was this incredibly handsome, gentle, intelligent man, and to my thinking, I was fat, ugly, and stupid. Nor did he empathize with my insecurities.

"After all, I married you," he would tell me. "Isn't that enough?"

Those words seemed so cold to me, and I became convinced Don would leave me sooner or later. How could I possibly keep him? The only way I knew to make sure I'd always have a part of Don was to have his child. Maybe I'd even be lucky enough to have a son who would grow up to look and be just like Don. Of course, that child would love me as his mother, and no one would ever be able to take him away.

So once again I took life into my hands, manipulating as only I could. In March 1971, I gave birth to a third son. We named him Donald after his daddy. His middle name was Dustin, and we called him Dusty. He was such a beautiful, perfect baby boy. At the time, I didn't give God the credit. But when I looked at this child, I had a glimmer that there just might be a God after all. How could I explain otherwise how perfect my baby son was and exactly what I'd asked for? It did seem to be more than just coincidence.

Looking down at my beautiful son's angelic little face, my heart swelled with love, and I felt confidence pierce through my insecurities. Finally, I'd done something right. Dusty would always be my son, and Don would never leave that child. He and Dusty very quickly developed a bond that went beyond just father and son, and I knew then that I had Don forever because his love for his son trumped everything in his life.

Dusty was truly my little miracle.

CHAPTER ELEVEN

DON'T CRY, MARK!

After Dusty's birth, my renewed self-confidence helped me lose weight, fix my hair more attractively, and do my best to compete with the women who seemed to just pop up in our lives. I had my defense in knowing Don would never leave his son, and I'd learned to fight for what I wanted.

The bar maid Charlene continued to flirt with Don, and I dreaded every night he went to work. Some of my female acquaintances didn't even try to hide their feelings for Don. One attractive woman named Sharon was always asking me about things he liked. At a dance we were all attending, she and Don danced together repeatedly while I watched from the sidelines. A woman standing next to me commented, "Aren't they a lovely couple."

That was *my* husband she was talking about! Another acquaintance, Missy, would constantly insert herself into the spotlight with Don. On one outing we all took together, she grabbed Don's arm as we were walking down the street, usurping my place as his wife. When we stopped for a drink, she sat on his lap. She monopolized conversation with him, piling on the compliments.

At another dance, the beautiful wife of a rich philanthropist flirted with Don, and he danced one song after another with her. She was so beautiful with her tiny black dress and perfect body. I sat there in my own dowdy clothes, knowing I just couldn't measure up. The pain was unimaginable. This was the kind of woman Don should be with, not me.

To make matters worse, our finances were grim to say the least. I'd wanted to help Don with his new business and spend more time with him, so I'd resigned from my job at the auto dealership. But the tavern was not doing well financially, and I became increasingly upset that I'd left such a prestigious job to basically work as a barmaid. Don's partner had another job, so most of the time Don and I were left to run the business on our own.

To juggle caring for the boys, Don worked nights and I worked days except for Monday evening. Every Monday the tavern offered a huge crab feed, and it was always a packed house. That was the only time I ever left the boys with a sitter.

One Monday evening in April 1971 as I left the house to drive over to the tavern, I could smell fragrant blossoms beginning to bloom on flowering trees along the street. A warm breeze drifted around me like a soft blanket, unusual for a spring evening in Seattle. What a contrast to the dark, dingy, smoke-filled tavern when I walked inside. As always on Monday evenings, it was very crowded. The kitchen was behind on orders, so I buckled down to moving as fast as I could.

We hadn't been working too long when the phone rang. Typically when we were this busy, we would just let any calls go. But Don picked up the phone. When I glanced over again, he was still on the phone. He seemed deeply involved in the conversation, a hand over one ear to hear better over the noise of tavern customers. I couldn't believe he would take time to talk to someone when we were so busy.

Then I realized his face was pale and intense. A shudder of premonition went down my spine at his expression. Hanging up the phone, he headed toward me at a full run. I could hear him speaking as he grabbed my arm so hard it hurt and pulled me toward the door. But the words just didn't make sense to me. "Mark has been hit by a car."

Then as what he'd said sank in, my legs went weak and heavy like lead weights. My head was spinning, and a horrible, dizzying fog choked out everything around me. How was this even possible? When I'd left the boys not an hour earlier, they'd been safely laughing and playing indoors with little Dusty, who was still an infant. I'd held Mark's little face in my hands as I kissed him goodbye, saying, "Mark, I love you so much."

"I love you too, Mommy." Beautiful green eyes smiling up at me, Mark had playfully stuck out his tongue and run off laughing.

Turning my terrified gaze to my husband, I demanded, "Where did this happen?"

"Roxbury Street," Don responded.

I was stunned. Roxbury Street was two full blocks from our house, a very busy four-lane boulevard with fast-moving traffic. The boys were forbidden to go anywhere near there. What had they been doing outside, and why hadn't the babysitter been watching them?

I learned much later that the babysitter had sent Chris and Mark to a gas station store on Roxbury Street to purchase cigarettes for her. She was only about fifteen years old, and we had no idea she smoked. Chris was nine and Mark seven years old, so perhaps she felt they were responsible enough to walk the two blocks while she stayed with baby Dusty.

But with his mischievous, playful nature, Mark hadn't waited for a break in traffic to cross the street. He kept jumping out toward the cars as though about to dart into the traffic. When one car stopped for him, he took this as a signal that it was safe to run across the street. As he did so, a car approaching in the next lane hit Mark at full impact. He was thrown clear across the road, his tennis shoes knocked off in the impact.

Poor little Chris witnessed the entire thing. To this day, he can hear in his mind the horrible thud of the accident. On top of that, he was left alone to walk home and tell the babysitter what had just happened to his little brother.

We arrived at the hospital before the ambulance. Confused and terrified, I watched the medics lift out the gurney carrying my son's small body. As the medics rushed the gurney past us, I reached out as though I could help in some way. The spirited child I'd left such a short time earlier just lay there ashen and limp, his beautiful green eyes closed.

A doctor came running out to meet the ambulance. Glancing at me, he asked angrily, "How did this happen?"

Before I could reply, he turned and ran with the gurney into the emergency room. Don and I followed. We were directed to wait in a small room next to where the doctors were trying to save Mark's life. Saying I felt helpless doesn't begin to describe my emotions. Guilt and fear consumed me to the point that I was numb to everything happening around us.

Then the door opened, and a person dressed in scrubs said, "You might want to call someone from your church."

Church? What church? The only church I knew was Catholic because that's where my mother went. Don and I didn't go to church. We didn't pray. I didn't even know how to pray. Neither of us believed in God. We'd jokingly speak of *the big guy upstairs* or *Ralph*, referencing the clumsy carpenter on Green Acres, a popular sitcom then, since God is supposed to be the one who makes everything work.

But this was no joke. Don and I sat there hour after excruciating hour staring at the tile floor, afraid to speak, afraid to breathe. We couldn't even turn to each other for support as what was there to be said? It was the loneliest feeling imaginable. All we could do was believe Mark would live. That he might die was too horrible a thought to even entertain. It just couldn't happen.

A Catholic priest arrived wearing a purple sash around his neck and carrying the various items involved in administering last rites. The nurses started ushering him in to where Mark was still being helped by the doctors. I was furious since we weren't Catholic and hadn't asked for a priest.

"No, no, don't go in there!" I cried out. "He's not going to die. Go away. Leave him alone."

They all ignored my request, and the priest walked on into Mark's room, shutting me out. I guess someone who was Catholic on the medical staff was worried a dying child might be denied entrance into heaven without last rites so had called the priest. But I was outraged they would do this without parental permission.

Later, Mark was moved to an intensive care unit where we could see him through a glass window. His little body was so swollen he hardly looked human, and his shock of blonde hair had been shaved off due to massive brain injuries. I felt completely helpless, useless, unable to do anything to alleviate my precious son's pain.

Someone came to tell us that a brain specialist was flying in to examine Mark. People ran in and out of his room. Frightened, confused, and heartbroken, Don and I just kept sitting there hour after hour, unable to move or speak. The sounds of the hospital became familiar to us. We learned that when a voice cried out "Code Red, Code Red," it was a signal for doctors to rush into Mark's room. My heart jumped each time they used the defibrillator paddles to start Mark's heart. To this day, I can't bear to watch a movie that has paddles shocking someone's heart.

Twelve excruciating hours after the initial phone call, Don and I stood hand in hand staring out the hospital window at the traffic below. The sun had risen. A new day was beginning. Lights were coming on in nearby houses. People would be waking up and starting their normal day, getting ready for work, having breakfast, getting their children ready for school.

How many times had Don and I awakened to a new day refreshed and happy? We'd sipped our morning coffee and gone about our business without giving a thought to the tragedies playing out in the lives of others. Now in this very hospital, one tiny life was slipping away while others were beginning. As our beautiful little Mark struggled to stay alive, mothers were welcoming babies into this world.

Footsteps echoed as someone walked slowly toward us down the cold, empty hallway. Clutching Don's hand tightly, I kept my eyes staring straight ahead, unable to face whoever was approaching. I wanted to cover my ears because I knew what this person was going to say, and I refused to hear it. But I couldn't shut out the doctor's somber voice. "I'm so sorry. We did all we could, but we were not able to save your son."

"No! No!" A horrible dark cloud descended on me as my mind tried to deny what I'd just heard. There had to be a mistake. It couldn't be true.

We were led into the room where Mark lay pale and still. I was engulfed by horrible guilt. Why hadn't I been there to safeguard my precious son? I wanted to snatch him up in my arms and never let him go. He already felt cold, so I tucked the covers in around him as though that would warm him up. Leaning over to kiss him, I saw a tear in the corner of his eye. That crushed my heart.

"Don't cry, Markie, sweetheart," I whispered, tears pouring down my own cheeks. "Mommy is here. And I'm so, so sorry I wasn't there to protect you."

Chapter Twelve

More Than I Can Bear

Leaving Mark in that room with strangers was the hardest thing I had ever done. With Don's support, I managed to put one foot in front of the other toward the door. As we walked down the hallway, people were talking, laughing, and going about their day. Didn't they know my son had just died?

As we drove away from the hospital, I leaned my head against the cold glass window of the car. How could I go home and see Mark's things, his clothes, his toys, all the signs of his life? It would be more than I could bear.

We ended up just driving around aimlessly. My head was spinning, and grief sucked me down into a cold, dark hole. Mark wasn't coming back. This horrible, horrible nightmare was real. In one short day, we'd been thrust into a world of pain and loss I didn't know existed.

We didn't have God in our lives, so I had no hope that Mark was safely in a wonderful afterlife. Fury rose up inside of me when people told me, "He's with Jesus now."

How can they say that? I seethed inside angrily. *What does Jesus need with my son? How could Mark be better off with Jesus? Mark is dead. If there is a Jesus, I hate him for what he has allowed!*

I couldn't read a paper or watch the news because every time I'd see storms, wars, death, and other terrible things shattering innocent lives, I would become overwhelmed and angry. I knew such things happened, of course. I'd just never thought about them happening to us. Now I realized how much in life is totally out of one's control. That in itself was terrifying.

Most days, I sat looking out the window, frozen with grief. Somehow, I had to find the courage to go on for my other two sons, Chris and Dusty. I will never forget seeing Chris run to meet me when we finally arrived home from the hospital.

"Mommy, did you hear what happened to Mark?" he asked anxiously. "Is he going to be okay?"

I felt so helpless as I held this innocent child in my arms, knowing he'd relive the horror of what he'd witnessed for the rest of his life. "Chris, I'm so sorry, but the doctors couldn't fix Markie, and he won't be coming home."

At least Dusty was too young to remember other than stories others would tell. I wished I could block out my own painful memories. I was still a mom and wife, which meant getting up to face each new day. I didn't want Don and the boys to worry about me, so I felt I had to hide my grief, be strong, bear up under the torture. Don and I never spoke of what had happened. It was just too terrible to bring up. Instead, I turned my pain inward, and like a cancer, it started to devour me.

The hardest thing was having to face people. I never knew what to say, and it was impossible to smile because of the terrible guilt I felt. How could I smile? Mark was dead.

I'd never felt so alone. We lost most of our friends because we were just so pitiful to be around. I became very aware of how awkward it is for people to approach someone who is going through a difficult time.

What we didn't want was for people to act like nothing had happened. We needed them to just say sincerely, "I'm so sorry you're going through this." Or "I want you to know I care."

Instead, we received some of the most insensitive comments. One woman approached me to say, "Kathy, my aunt lost her son too."

Another asked, "Did you see the news about someone who lost six children in a fire?"

"Shut up!" I wanted to scream at them. "You have no idea what we're going through. Talking about other people's grief doesn't take my mind off Mark. It doesn't help, so just shut up!"

Only someone who has lost a child can possibly understand the terrible guilt I felt. We plan for the deaths of our parents. We even plan for our own demise. But we never expect our children to die before us. It's not the natural order of things. What should I even say when people asked how many children I had? In the end, I told people that I had three sons, but one was now an angel.

A month had passed, and I found it no easier to get out of bed each morning. Bills were starting to arrive in the mailbox. Funeral expenses, hospital bills, doctor bills all piled up. The flowers and cards never seemed to stop coming either. I grew to hate the smell of dying flowers, and the cards were so painful to open. *In Sympathy,* they would typically say. But I didn't want sympathy. I wanted my son back.

Then one day my heart skipped a beat as I open a card that read, "Dear Kathy, I just want you to know we are praying for you. Life can sometimes hand us very difficult things, and I'm so sorry for the loss of your precious son Mark. I know the pain you are suffering because the same thing happened to us several years ago."

I can't tell you what this short note from a perfect stranger meant to me. If this mother had survived her loss, maybe I could too. Showing it to my husband, I told him, "Oh Don, I haven't been convinced that I'll ever survive this pain. But she did. That's so encouraging."

Our local newspaper ran a short article about Mark's death. I sat there and read about my own son. How many times in the past had I read such articles about other people and been sure that could never happen to us? As weeks went by, the guilt, pain, isolation, and bitterness settled deeper and deeper into my heart. When people tried to console me or offered to pray for me, I just got angrier. If there was a God, I didn't want to hear about Him. Just look what He had done!

One day, there was a knock on the door. Slowly, I got up and opened the front door. There stood two nuns from the Catholic church a few blocks away.

"Hello," they started in. "We just came to tell you how sorry we are about your son and to give you a little hope."

I could already feel the anger rising in my darkened heart as they continued, "It's so reassuring to know your little son is with Jesus now."

"Jesus!" I screamed at them. "If you believe my son is with Jesus, then you are saying that Jesus kills little children. There is no God, and there is no hope!"

Slamming the door in their faces, I collapsed down on the floor sobbing. I was so angry, and all these well-meaning people praying for me and telling me about Jesus just threw me into deeper depression and despair. At that point, I don't think anyone could have reached me, no matter what they had to say. Looking back, I know their intentions were good. I'm sure they were praying for me and pleading my case before God.

Years later, Don and I ran into a young man, who quickly stopped us. "You are Mark's parents, aren't you?"

We were startled at his statement. Tears filling his eyes, the young man went on, "I was a classmate of Mark's. We were good friends. My life was never the same after he died. I grieved and had to go to counseling. I still miss him today."

As we stood there chatting and comparing some good memories of Mark, mixed emotions swept over me. I had never once thought about how others might have been affected by Mark's death.

By now, I'd gathered up Mark's clothing, which I took to the nearest Goodwill. But for months afterwards, I found myself looking at every young boy I saw to see if he might be wearing one of Mark's shirts or jacket. I'd go back to the Goodwill to check if any of his things were still there.

I knew this wasn't a healthy response. Maybe I was crazy for a while. I couldn't sleep more than three or four hours a night. I had constant thoughts of death and the morbid visions that came with those thoughts. I felt anxious all the time.

One day I was driving my car. When I came to one intersection, I noticed a sign showing a car hitting the stick figure of a person. It was probably meant to get people to watch out for pedestrians. But I was so emotionally impacted that I began blacking out and had to pull over.

I was also having horrible, vivid nightmares as I hadn't experienced since my abusive marriage with Al Wheeler. In one such nightmare, I'd been buried alive and could feel water seeping into my cold casket. I'd jerk myself awake with sweat running down my face.

In another nightmare, I was trying to get Mark to the funeral home. He was in a baby carriage, which at his age didn't fit. The rain was pouring down. I was trying to push the carriage over the wet grass, but its wheels kept sinking into the mud. I struggled and struggled, crying all the way. When I finally reached the door of the funeral home, I was informed that I had to take Mark to the mortuary first, and I was late.

"What's wrong with me?" I asked Don in a panic. Later I was diagnosed with PTSD.

Chapter Thirteen

Run, Run, Run!

A better question would be what *wasn't* wrong with me. My once-perfect life, marriage, and family continued to collapse as though my vow asking for one happy year before losing everything was indeed coming true. If Don and I had a lot of stress in our marriage before the accident, after Mark's death it became indescribably worse. We would get into an argument, and I would start crying. Before long, my sobbing would become uncontrollable, and I would realize I was crying about Mark, not the argument.

Our financial situation was horrendous. We owed many tens of thousands of dollars from the extraordinary efforts made to save Mark's life, a sum that would be equivalent to ten times that today. But we had no money. The tavern business was failing miserably, and I wasn't stable enough to work. Even if I'd wanted to return to my former job, I couldn't because the auto dealership had gone bankrupt due to some bad investments. Having bill collectors call and threaten us became an everyday occurrence.

Knowing our tight finances, our business partner's wife brought over some meat she'd picked up from her parents' farm.

I was so excited as we could not afford to buy meat. But when I opened the package, I could immediately smell the putrid stench of spoiled flesh.

Around that time, Don discovered that his business partner was stealing from the business. His wife did all the bookkeeping, and we had no clue what was going on financially. Or even if the tavern had really been doing so badly rather than this couple having skimmed off the profits. I had to wonder if her unexpected meat offering simply reflected a guilty conscience. I tried to give her the credit that she hadn't realized the meat was spoiled.

Several months after Mark's funeral, the phone rang early one morning. The caller was from the funeral services company that had provided Mark's headstone. "We are calling on behalf of Aurora Monument. You have already received four notices about nonpayment of the grave marker you purchased. If the outstanding balance is not immediately paid in full, there will be no other option but to repossess the item in question."

After everything else we were going through, I was utterly devastated that anyone would threaten to take my precious Mark's grave marker. What possible good would a used grave marker be to these people? In the end, no one ever took the grave marker, and I never found out why. Maybe the bill collectors were just trying to scare us, or maybe Don found some way to pay for it. I just didn't know.

It didn't help that Don and I were barely talking to each other. We couldn't share our grief, so we both just shoved it deeper and deeper inside. I had such a feeling of hopelessness and no desire to continue living. I rarely ventured out of the house. Leaving Chris and Dusty for even a few minutes struck terror into my heart. I was so frightened something terrible would happen to them too. I trusted no one, so I made sure to drive Chris to school and pick him up every day. Trying to shield and protect my two remaining sons became my sole life's purpose.

But that didn't dissolve my terrible guilt over losing Mark. I've read somewhere in Freudian psychology about the *death instinct*. This is an instinct that makes a person repress all desire for pleasurable things in life and cultivate instead a desire for self-annihilation, which leads to destructive behavior and even suicide. It is associated with feelings of guilt.

I had so much of that. Flashbacks of times when I had failed Mark as a mother kept coming to mind. One of these involved a scar on Mark's little finger. He'd cut it on a toy car, and I'd bandaged it as best I could. He needed stitches, but we couldn't afford a doctor. Now I felt tortured by the thought of that disfigured little finger.

I found myself developing personality traits that were harmful. I couldn't stand anyone who wasted my time. People in department stores who talked on the phone instead of helping me. Wait staff at a restaurant who ignored me. Long hold times on the phone. All these sent me into a tantrum. *Don't waste my time*, became my mantra.

As I evaluated my reactions to these takers of time, I realized that my painful circumstances with Mark were responsible. I'd had just seven short years with him before he died. It seemed to me I'd wasted that time and hadn't been the best mom I could be. I'd been so busy trying to support our family as a single mom there wasn't time to sit and hold Mark when he was frustrated and lonely. Now my arms ached to hold him just one more time. But he was gone forever, and all that remained was my guilt.

As the months passed, life remained on hold for Don and me. It was difficult for us to go out anywhere. We weren't much fun to be around. What could we talk to others about? How could we explain the sadness in our eyes? We'd lost most of our friends, and the art of conversation had left us.

If we'd only had a church family or pastor or anyone to guide us through this terrible time. But we had no one. So we just withdrew from each other and from other people, each of us dealing with our grief and despair the best we knew how.

By now my depression had grown far beyond what might be considered normal even when dealing with the agonizing loss of a child. I really needed help. I saw doctors, but painful experience left me unable to trust sharing my true feelings with them. One doctor chided me for concentrating on negative emotions and told me I needed to look at the positive times I'd had with Mark. That's what Mark would want.

"Maybe so," I told him bluntly. "But you, doctor, have never lost a child."

On at least three occasions, I considered taking my own life. The first time was sitting on our bed with a loaded gun. I didn't want to die but couldn't stand the pain any longer. Thankfully, I didn't go through with it. The second time, I took sleeping pills, not enough to kill me, but I slept for two days and had a terrible hangover.

On a third occasion, Don and I were staying in a hotel. Our room was on the fourth floor. Crawling out onto the window ledge, I sat there with my feet dangling over the ledge. I could see cars coming in and out of the hotel drive far below. It suddenly occurred to me that if I leaned forward just a few inches, all my pain would be gone.

I wasn't thinking straight or considering the consequences to my family. At that moment, there just seemed no other way out. But as I leaned forward, I had a sudden vision of my son Chris just as clear as life.

"Mommy, don't!" he called urgently.

In shock, I backed off and hurriedly climbed down off the ledge. My mind cleared enough to comprehend what it would have done to him if I'd taken my own life. I realize that some are not so lucky, and depression has taken their lives. For their families, I truly grieve. It is such a terrible disease of our spirit.

Do people who take their own life automatically go to hell? I don't think so. After all, God did not leave me in hell but gave me a second chance and the opportunity for repentance. I believe Jesus can reveal Himself to people during the dying process and that they may be given opportunity to repent.

Is this a free ticket for those contemplating suicide to go ahead with their plan? Absolutely not! The night I was on that ledge and saw the vision of my precious young son, I was able to look into the pain of the families of suicide victims. The tragedy never leaves them, and we don't have the right to hurt others that way.

One day, Don's partner in the tavern business came to us with a proposal. He would pull out of the partnership, giving us the business outright. Don and I were so naïve. His partner knew the tavern was headed for bankruptcy, especially after all the money he and his wife had siphoned from the business. He just wanted out before things imploded. But Don accepted the offer. Building a sports bar was his dream, so he continued to fight and try to save the business.

Then came that horrible evening several months after the accident when some friends of Don's invited us to a party. The purpose for the party was to celebrate the opening of a new business by one of Don's acquaintances. I begged Don not to make me go out. It was still just too soon. I didn't want to leave Chris and Dusty with a babysitter. How could I enjoy a party when I knew I would be frantic the whole time over their safety? But Don insisted, so I reluctantly made arrangements for a babysitter, got dressed, and we left the house.

We never made it to the party. To this day, I couldn't even tell you how our quarrel started or what it was about. But as I shared in the first chapter, I lashed out at Don while he was driving with all the fury that was in me. In response, he swung his arm as forcefully as he could to push me away. His fist struck my back so hard that I fell over against my side of the car.

I was stunned and not just because of the pain. I'd endured so much physical abuse from Al Wheeler, but my wonderful, gentle Don had never laid an unkind hand on me, and I'd never dreamed he could. Straightening up, I asked Don to just take me home. He immediately turned the car around. Once we got home, Don rushed into the bathroom. Leaned over the sink, he began splashing cold water on his face. I could see the grief on his face, and I knew how sorry he was for what had happened. But what could I say? How could we make all the hurt go away?

From a very young age, my fallback when hurt by life's raw, painful episodes was to run as far and fast as I could. And taking my miserable self as far away from Don as possible was all I could think of right now. So that's what I did, even though it was dark and raining outside. I knew Don would certainly make me stop if he heard me. So I retrieved the car keys and slipped out the front door as quietly as possible.

At this point, I wasn't aware of the injury I'd sustained earlier in the car. I learned later that Don's blow had struck my back right where the liver is located, causing the membrane that protects the jelly-like interior of the liver to burst, which in turn caused massive internal bleeding. Looking back, I'm sure adrenaline had kicked in and was masking the pain.

Jumping into the car, I shoved it into gear and drove off, squealing the tires on the pavement. Don came rushing out of the house. I heard him yelling for me to stop, but I pushed the accelerator to the floor. Glancing into the rearview mirror, I saw him standing in the driveway in a posture of total frustration. The road was blurred by my tears, and I wondered how much worse life could get. As I drove into the dark night, I wished it would swallow me up forever.

Then I started to notice a throbbing pain deep inside my chest. At first I tried to ignore it, but the pain got worse by the minute. Also, I was so distraught I couldn't tell if the pain I felt was caused by an actual injury or a broken heart. But it soon became difficult to breath, and I realized something was terribly wrong.

Stopping the car by the side of the road, I carefully slid out of the driver's seat, hanging onto the car door to keep from falling. I was high on a hillside overlooking Seattle, but the bright city lights below seemed just a blur of color. The pain had become so bad that I was hunched over. Cars sped by me, barely missing my opened door. Horns honked. People yelled at me. But no one bothered to stop and offer help.

By now all I could think of was the dreadful pain. Breathing was so difficult that I loosened my clothing. I knew I had to get home before I lost consciousness. I finally gathered enough strength to get back behind the wheel and merge into the speeding traffic. What was wrong with me? What would Don think when he saw me in such a mess?

The cars on the freeway as I drove carefully home were just a haze of color, the dark, rainy night swallowing them up one by one. Fearful of fainting, I rolled down the windows and let the freezing rain hit my face. Somehow, I made it home. Now I had to face Don. He would be angry, and who could blame him. Would he believe me when I told him I was in dire need of help and needed to get to a hospital?

Don must have heard the car's return because he opened the front door as I pulled into the driveway. His stance made clear he was very angry. I almost fell out of the car. My clothes were all soaked and undone, my hair windblown and wet from the rain. I could hardly walk so I just staggered toward the front door, hunched over like a wounded animal. My entire focus was getting inside to the phone so I could call 911.

"Kathy, what are you doing?" Don demanded anxiously as I pushed my way past him. "What's wrong?"

"I need a doctor right away. I'm going to call an ambulance." But by now I could no longer even stagger. I fell to my hands and knees, still crawling desperately in the direction of the phone.

Then Don crouched down beside me, and I felt his strong hands help me to my feet. Relief washed over me as I saw that he believed me and was going to help. His arms around me felt like angels' wings as he guided me to the car and settled me inside. He drove me to the hospital. That is where I had the death-to-life experience I told you about in chapter one of this story.

CHAPTER FOURTEEN

SECOND CHANCES

My body lay unbreathing and without a pulse on the operating table. But my spirit continued to fall helplessly into the darkness, enveloped by the agony of pain and tortured by the cries of others falling into oblivion around me.

Then suddenly I realized I wasn't falling anymore. In an instant, the torture just stopped. I felt myself being hurled backwards out of the depths of hell, back through the long, dark tunnel, and down towards my lifeless body. I felt bewilderment, perplexed that I was coming back to life.

You have likely heard the phrase *the will to live* or *giving up the ghost*. There comes a time during the dying process when you can actually see the person give up that *will to live* and subsequently die. When people speak of someone who has *given up the ghost*, they are saying that the spirit has left the physical body and the person is dead.

I can now testify to the accuracy of both these phrases. Just as my *ghost* had left my body, leaving me without brain function or pulse, so now I could feel a renewed will to live as though I'd crossed an actual threshold back into my physical body. It was an incredible sensation I will never forget. One moment, the desire to be with God and remain in that peaceful, amazing place called heaven was pulling me one direction. Then a yearning to live was pulling me in the other direction.

As I reentered my body, the will to live was like blood being transfused into my veins. With a surge, my lungs filled with air, and I could breathe again. I felt a sudden thrill that I was alive. I would see Don and my sons again.

But I was totally mystified as to why I was coming back to life. It bewildered me that God could forgive all the anger, rebellion, and unbelief I'd lived with for so many years and give me of all people a second chance at life. Also, I was deeply thankful to have been rescued from that horrible experience of hell. But I didn't want to leave behind the incredible experience I'd had of feeling the powerful, glorious, loving presence of our Lord God Almighty.

"I can't go back to consciousness now that I know the incredible peace, love, beauty, and tranquility of being with You," I cried out to God. "This afterlife of a real heaven living in eternity with You is so amazing I was drawn to it even above my love for my sons and husband and everything else on earth. How can I leave all that behind to go back?"

That moment was when I received the only verbal communication I've had with God as a mighty, majestic voice conveyed to me the command, "*BRING PEOPLE TO ME!*"

I knew then that I'd been given a task. That was why I was being sent back. And indeed who better to point people to redemption than a sinner brought back from the depths of hell by an all-loving, forgiving God? I am still brought to tears just thinking about where I've come from and where God has brought me.

That was the last awareness I had before awaking from the anesthetic with machines hooked to every part of my body. The lights of the operating room were like looking into a bright sun. Masked strangers were working feverishly over my pale, limp frame. I could hear many different voices.

I eventually learned that bursting the protective covering, the *balloon* that surrounded my liver, had basically shattered it into pieces. Repairing such an injury is like trying to sew Jell-O together. In the mid-1960s, there were no MRI or CT scans available, so my attending physician, a brilliant, young surgeon named Dr. Uri Breda, had gone into surgery with no knowledge of what to expect. I was later informed that at that time in medical history only about ten percent of patients survived such an operation.

Certainly, there was no reason barring a miracle why I'd survived. As I regained consciousness, there was no doubt in my conscious mind that I had died. Now I was alive again, and though I was in terrible pain, I kept trying desperately to tell everyone around me what had happened.

"Let me go back!" I was screaming. "I want to see heaven. I want to be with God."

The doctors ignored my verbal ramblings and kept working on me. When I was wheeled into recovery, Don was there. Grabbing his arm, I tried desperately to tell him what had happened to me. "Don, you must believe me. I died! I know there is a God, and I was actually in hell!"

Don's face was drawn, and he looked so bewildered and tired. But he gently leaned down and said, "I believe you."

And I could tell that he did. But it seemed like he was the only one. When I tried to explain my death-to-life experience to others, their first reaction was typically to assume my brain had been deprived of oxygen, which had caused hallucinations. After all, I'd gone into cardiac arrest on the operating table. My heart had stopped beating long enough for the doctors to declare me clinically dead and remove the anesthesia mask along with other equipment. All that was in my medical records.

The remainder of my time in the hospital was grueling. I had a burning, tender scar running down the center of my chest from the surgery. My condition was still so precarious a nurse was assigned to sit by my bedside twenty-hours a day. Sometime after the surgery, my lungs began filling with fluid. Rushing into my room, Dr. Breda told me resolutely, "I'm not going to lose you now!"

Bending me over the bed tray, he thrust a huge needle through my back into my lungs, then proceeded to draw out the fluid. The pain was excruciating, but the procedure proved successful. Even so, my recovery was touch-and-go. To make the situation worse, my father, who had shown me so little love or concern, threatened to have my dear, loving husband arrested for attempted murder if I died.

Thankfully, that didn't happen, and I was eventually discharged. When I met with Dr. Breda for follow-up care, I told him a little more of my experience while I'd been clinically dead, then asked. "So can you explain what happened to me?"

Dr. Breda looked pensive as he responded, "All I can tell you is that the anesthesiologist said that we'd lost you. There was no brain activity and no heartbeat. In truth, I don't know what happened to you. I just know that one minute you were clinically dead and the next you were alive again."

I persisted in my questioning. "But couldn't my experience have just been a lack of oxygen when there was no blood going to the brain? I've heard that lack of oxygen can cause people to have hallucinations of bright lights and being pulled through a tunnel. Or maybe some sort of nightmare brought on by the anesthesia?"

Dr. Breda shook his head. "Oxygen deprivation is quite different. When the brain is deprived of oxygen, people can indeed experience bright flashing lights or a flurry of fragmented, unorganized images. Not the clear, vivid, organized sequence of events you've described. As for the anesthesia, you were given a general anesthetic, which causes the brain to be insensitive to any stimuli. So it's unlikely you'd be experiencing anything like what you've described while under anesthetic and without a heartbeat."

I left Dr. Breda's office convinced that what happened to me had really happened. This had been no dream or nightmare. I'd had nightmares before and dreams both good and bad. And I'd abused alcohol enough to know what hallucinations felt like. This was much different. My experience had been as real as the doctor's office in which I was sitting.

Don never once doubted what I'd told him or dismissed my experience as the result of my very complicated surgery or anesthetic. He just seemed to know as I now knew that God does exist. This was even more amazing considering neither of us had any belief in God prior to this experience. We'd laughed at the notion of the Almighty. We'd mocked God. Anyone trying to comfort us after Mark's death with words about a loving deity had just provoked anger. I wanted to know nothing of a God who'd killed my son.

Now all that was erased, and I knew beyond any doubt that this Supreme Being did exist. Even more wonderful was that I also knew beyond doubt that my son Mark was with this supreme, loving, compassionate God in a place of total, incredible, unexplainable love, peace, and joy. And I now had the hope of one day seeing my son again and being with him in that amazing place forever.

CHAPTER FIFTEEN

BEYOND THE GRIEF

Don and I had been in terrible financial straits since Mark's accident. So many wonderful surgeons and other medical personnel had heroically tried to save Mark's life. But though they failed, they still had to charge us. Now similar bills were coming in from the heroic efforts of keeping me alive. The tavern continued to lose money. We finally had no choice but to declare bankruptcy. The bank stepped in and repossessed everything we had except the roof over our heads.

Losing the dream into which he'd poured so much hard work, commitment, and love was a sword-thrust to the core of Don's heart, making him feel as though he'd failed as a man. I knew how deeply hurt he was, but though I wanted to comfort him, I didn't know how.

We now had no income at all. Food became increasingly scarce. The grocery store wouldn't accept my checks, and I couldn't blame them. It was a trip backwards to when the boys and I were living in the housing projects, broke, and unable to even buy groceries. Don went back to working in real estate for a friend who had built a very successful company. I focused on trying to regain my physical health. The surgical scar running down the middle of my chest was a daily reminder of my horrible ordeal and near-death experience.

Then came another major life upheaval. Just months after my own death-to-life experience, my father died suddenly of a massive heart attack at just fifty-three years of age. Despite the unloving relationship I'd had with him, I grieved, if only for the loss of any hope that he'd change and become the affectionate, caring father I'd always longed for.

By this time, my younger brother was married and had a daughter. My younger sister was college age. While attending the University of Washington, she'd been chosen as an exchange student in France. She loved her experience there and eventually made France her home. After my father's death, my mother inherited quite a bit of money. She used her inheritance to travel all over Europe with my younger sister and brother. I didn't begrudge her this, but when she'd spent it all, she returned home penniless. With my siblings moved away, I became her caregiver, a responsibility that lasted for the rest of my mother's life.

But in all these difficult challenges and upheavals, there was one big change for the good. If everything else in my life was uncertain, I now knew for sure that God did exist, and my heart wanted nothing more than to draw closer to Him. I knew nothing about God, religion, or the Bible other than the blind faith I'd had as a child and what little I'd learned attending the Catholic church with my mother.

I decided that going to church would be a good start. Catholicism was the only religion I was familiar with, and there was a Catholic church a few blocks away, the same one from which I'd received a visit from two nuns after Mark's death. They held mass every morning at six a.m. except days when they had funerals. I began attending mass there every day it was open.

But just as when I was a child, I really wasn't learning anything about the God I'd encountered in my near-death experience. This was now after Vatican 2, and the Catholic church around the world had begun offering mass in the vernacular language rather than Latin, which in the United States meant English. But other than the liturgy of mass, the church I attended still offered no in-depth teaching about God, Jesus, or the contents of the Bible.

If I was to draw closer to God as I yearned, I recognized that I needed more teaching than Catholicism was providing me. The wife of the friend whose real estate company Don now worked for was a committed Christian. We became friends, and I told her of my near-death experience. We met for lunch almost daily and talked about Jesus. She attended a nearby evangelical church and invited me there. I continued attending Catholic mass every morning at six a.m. but also began attending the evangelical church on Wednesday nights and Sunday mornings.

One thing I learned at this church was how important it was to give your mind and body to Jesus. I wasn't sure what that was all about, but one morning while at six a.m. mass, something just came over me. There were never more than five or six people in attendance at that hour. On this particular morning, there was just one other elderly woman. After mass, she began praying the fourteen stations of the cross on her way to the exit. This left me alone in the church sanctuary, so I threw myself down at the altar. Lying flat on the cold stone floor, I began crying out to God.

"God, I believe in You with all my heart. Please come to me, live through me, and guide my life. I am a sinner. But whatever time I have left on earth, I give to You. Please, God, take my life and do what You will with it."

The most wonderful peace came over me, and I could feel God's unmistakable presence, the same awesome, powerful, loving presence I'd encountered in my death-to-life experience. All those church phrases I hadn't understood before—asking Jesus/God into your heart, being saved, being born again—now made absolute sense because this was exactly what I'd just experienced.

From that point on, I noticed some different things happening. For instance, I could feel other people's emotions. One day as I was walking through the grocery store, a woman brushed by me, and I immediately sensed she was in desperate need of help. I could feel her sadness. I knew God was calling me to do something, but I had no idea what.

Having the death-to-life experience caused an immediate change that has continued to prove stronger than any other profound experience in my life. I never felt special or chosen or that it was some kind of miracle. Rather, there was a sense of having been given a gift. Not a special gift of knowledge or ability to foresee the unknown but a deep capacity of compassion for the unloved and for reaching out to lost, lonely people who have no hope.

All that said, my newfound belief in God continued to leave me somewhat mystified as to why God had allowed me to live. I knew I didn't deserve a second chance, especially with the ungodly life I'd led, mocking God's name and staying so angry with those who believed in Him. I knew I didn't deserve God's forgiveness. The concept of Jesus taking all of our sins to the cross was foreign to me.

And yet, God's grace was extended to me. This gift was not given because of my level of faith or merit or effort but because of Christ's generous, sufficient sacrifice on our behalf. I am alive today and not burning in the agony of hell because of God's grace.

For the first time in my life, I began reading and studying the Bible. I found it very confusing at first. I didn't understand biblical history and customs or why the writers of this wonderful book had written a New Testament. Wasn't the old one good enough? And what was with all the numbers? But I just tried to stay focused. When I came to words that touched my heart, I would underline them. One passage especially seemed written just for me.

> To you, Lord, I called; to the Lord I cried for mercy: "What is gained if I am silenced, if I go down to the pit? Will the dust praise you? Will it proclaim your faithfulness? Hear, Lord, and be merciful to me; Lord, be my help."
>
> —Psalm 30:8-9

Wow! I felt that God's Holy Spirit guided me to those words. Bible research showed me that *the pit* was referring to Hades or hell. My memory brought a flashback of falling into that terrible pit during my near-death experience.

Though *Holy Spirit* was another term that rather scared me at first. Having only believed in a physical world I could see and touch all around me, I wasn't sure I wanted to be a part of a world than involved *spirit* beings and unseen forces. While I was now attending church, reading the Bible, and totally committed to Jesus Christ, I was like a newborn baby and still very fragile in my walk with God.

I came to understand that the Holy Spirit is my protector (John 14:15-31; 16:13-15) and that Satan is constantly sweeping this earth in search of vulnerable souls that he can swallow up and destroy (1 Peter 5:8). He hates you and me. There is a war going on for our souls between the forces of good and evil (Ephesians 6:10-12), and it is the Holy Spirit who gives us the power to resist (Ephesians 6:17). I read about the spiritual armor God provides for this battle— the belt of truth, breastplate of righteousness, shield of faith, helmet of salvation, and sword of the Spirit (Ephesians 6:13-17).

One day while sitting in church, I was just thinking about how much God had changed my life when I had a vision of being in a huge marble room with an enormous throne. I believe this was the throne of God. I didn't see God, but I saw myself lying face down before the throne. Then a huge golden sword was lowered to touch the top of my head. As the sword was raised back up, it lifted me to my feet.

In my vision, the sword was then handed to me. I somehow knew God was calling me to fight in that spiritual war and that I'd been given the sword to use it in the battle against evil. In this formative point of my walk with God, I was more like a baby taking its first steps than a warrior wielding a powerful weapon.

I stumbled and fell many times. But I always got up, and I have continued that spiritual fight to this very day.

One question I still pondered were the words I'd heard God audibly speak as the will to live entered back into my body during my near-death experience. *Bring people to Me!* What did that mean? As I read the Bible, I found so many passages that said the same thing.

Therefore go and make disciples of all nations.

—Matthew 28:30

Bring people to Me!

Go into all the world and preach the good news to all creation.

—Mark 16:15

Bring people to Me!

Let your light shine before others, that they may see your good deeds and glorify your Father in heaven.

—Matthew 5:16

Bring people to Me!

But you will receive power when the Holy Spirit comes on you; and you will be my witnesses . . . to the ends of the earth.

—Acts 1:8

Bring people to Me!

Always be prepared to give an answer to everyone who asks you to give the reason for the hope that you have.

—1 Peter 3:15

Bring people to Me!

Passages like these drew me deeper and deeper into studying the Bible. I also felt a deep, overwhelming desire to be in church, praying and worshiping God. I knew from what horrible destiny I had been saved. While Don was still not attending church with me, he encouraged me to attend. I always left an empty seat next to me and constantly prayed that Don would be there at my side someday.

Chapter Sixteen

A Chair Filled

I was getting physically stronger and made the choice to go back to work. Finding another auto dealership owned by a man named Bill Pierre, I explained to him what I'd done for Mr. Grant and assured him that I could really help his business by increasing car sales and boosting customer satisfaction. He hired me and gave me an office right next to his.

Once again, I was a manager and driving a new car. The pay was also better than I'd earned at the prior dealership. I'd made great friends in the evangelical church I was attending, including the pastor and his wife, Gary and Julie. Between my job, family, and going to church, life took on an entirely new, fun, and exciting direction.

My return to work was greatly eased by a dear, saintly neighborhood woman who volunteered to watch Dusty. She adored him and was constantly buying toys and other things for him. Dusty was very happy with her loving care. I can remember him asking me why I couldn't make toast like Mrs. Travis. Chris was in school most of the day and could walk over to Mrs. Travis's home if he got home before Don or I did. With that, I felt comfortable leaving the boys to return to work.

My relationship with God continued to develop. I read everything I could find about my Christian faith. I was now in a Bible-believing church under the guidance of a good pastor, and I was so hungry to learn about God that I attended every worship service, revival meeting, and other church events I could. For the first year, I continued attending the Catholic church as well. But one day while sitting in morning mass, I felt the Holy Spirit telling me that I should leave the Catholic church and place myself under just one pastor's teaching, so I did.

After that, it seemed every spare moment was spent praying, learning, and worshiping my newfound Savior. Prayer had at first been hard for me. Just sitting there talking to God seemed the most boring thing to do, and what I had to say felt so trivial compared to starving people, devastation, war, and all the huge problems God must be busy dealing with. I began hosting a women's prayer group at our house and quite honestly found myself falling asleep during the long prayers and wishing they'd just go home.

But I loved worshipping God. Singing songs of praise, lifting my arms to Jesus in surrender and thanksgiving for all He'd done in my life came naturally to me like a child singing *Jesus Loves Me.* I soon realized worship was a form of prayer. Just talking to God as a friend was prayer. Pouring out my wounded spirit and broken heart was prayer. In time, prayer became as natural for me as breathing.

One afternoon at a women's meeting, the speaker stated that she felt God had words of encouragement for some of us. Oh my! I was sure she must be speaking about me. After all, I had been saved from hell! Hmm, can you see a little spark of pride there?

As the speaker walked around the room, I felt God's presence speaking to me strongly. *If she comes to you, lie prostrate on the floor before Me.*

Here I was in a new white suit, and God was asking me to get down on the floor? I tried to ignore God's voice in my mind, but that just didn't work. Suddenly, I felt a hand on my shoulder. It was the speaker's. God's voice in my mind became louder. *Bow down before Me!*

With that, I fell to the floor in obedience to God, crying out loud, "Raca! Raca! Raca!"

You must believe me that I had no idea at the time what the word *raca* meant. But I knew God had placed that word on my tongue so it must have significance. I also knew God was working on an attitude of pride in me. A Bible word search showed me *raca* was an Aramaic word that meant worthless. In fact, it is only used once in the Bible in the Sermon on the Mount, where Jesus warns against using such an insult against others (Matthew 5:22).

So without even knowing what the word meant, I was crying out to God from my spirit that I was worthless and had no purpose without God. In truth, I was really begging God to forgive my sin of pride. What a great lesson I learned that day about pride. I know it sounds strange, but that really happened.

These lessons from God came one after another, and with each lesson I grew closer to God. I pray that this continues until the day my life on earth is over and God calls me home. Hopefully, I will have lived the life that God created me to live. I pray that God will guide me and escort me all the way to heaven as we read in the Psalms:

You guide me with your counsel, and afterward you will take me into glory.

—Psalm 73:24

Don saw the dramatic change in me from the person I'd been prior to my near-death experience. I'd been curious as to how he would respond to God after being by my side during surgery and afterwards. He hadn't felt the power and peace of God and the horrid pain of hell as I had. So why should he believe? How would anyone respond if a loved-one woke up from surgery to say they'd been to hell, then immediately went from being a complete atheist to an on-fire Christian?

Of course, Don knew something had happened because of the profound transformation that occurred in me. While he didn't immediately follow my lead, he soon began coming to church with me. In my zeal for knowing God more, I pulled him from one church to another, desperately trying to get him to believe as I did.

He went to the Catholic church with me, and though he rarely attended mass, he would go to the horseraces with our parish priest and call Bingo at church. Since the first church I'd attended was Catholic and my mother was Catholic, I decided it was important to have our civil courthouse marriage sanctified by the Catholic church. This proved quite difficult and cost four hundred dollars, equivalent to four thousand today. But I was determined and finally succeeded.

At the same time, I was also dragging Don to my friend's evangelical church where people spoke in tongues and raised their hands when they prayed. I know this must have been very confusing for him. It helped that Pastor Gary was very athletic and interested in sports just like Don. This became an immediate bond between them, and we became very close friends with Pastor Gary and his wife Julie. We had so much fun with them skiing, attending baseball game together, and other outings.

But Don's walk with God was his own, and no one can force belief onto another person. We can't drag them to the altar. All I could do was pray. There were so many nights when I laid my hands on Don's head as he slept and prayed that God would touch him and draw him.

It took several years of constant prayer and believing, but finally the day came when Don was ready to find his own path to God and follow Him. One Sunday during an altar call, Don responded and went forward. As Pastor Gary laid hands on Don and prayed over him, Don asked for God's forgiveness for his sins, placed his faith in Jesus Christ as his Savior, and committed his life to God. A short time later, he was baptized.

As with my own conversion, that day was a no-turning-back experience in Don's life. He entered into a wonderful relationship with God and has followed God faithfully ever since. The empty seat I'd always saved for Don was now filled, and what a thrill to have him sitting in that seat next to me, reaching for my hand each time there was prayer.

CHAPTER SEVENTEEN

A WOMAN'S VISION IN A MAN'S WORLD

One night in 1973, I had a dream. Or maybe it really was a vision from the Holy Spirit. I saw myself starting a business, and the dream showed me exactly how to do it. When I woke up and told Don what I wanted to do, my extreme excitement almost knocked him over.

So how did I start a business? By now I knew the names of most car dealerships in Seattle. These are typically a two-part business. They sell cars, usually both new and used, and they have a service department. My proposal was to do for other car dealerships what I'd done for Mr. Grant and Mr. Pierre. All I needed were the repair orders from the service department.

Once I had that information, I could phone customers and thank them for their business. I could check the repair order to see if the mechanics had flagged additional work needed immediately or in the near future. Rather than have the car break down or be taken elsewhere for service, I could suggest the customer have the work done at the dealership's service department, increasing revenues. I could also check the mileage to see if customers might be ready to trade this car in for a newer one.

At the same time, as I'd pioneered in my previous jobs, I could gather any complaints of poor service from the customers to pass on to the dealers so they could improve their customer satisfaction. This included following up with customers who had acquired new or used cars from that dealership to thank them and make sure all was going well with their purchase.

The advantage to the auto dealership of having an outside entity like me making the calls was that I wouldn't have any personal involvement with their employees. That ensured I'd be totally unbiased in my reports and just tell it like the customer said. The dealer would also be spared the hassle of hiring an employee to do this job who might or might not know what they were doing.

I made my first appointment with an auto dealer to find out if this program would be of interest to him. He almost came over the desk wanting to sign up. Right there I knew we were on to something big. That was the beginning of Customer Research, Inc., and also the beginning of the customer satisfaction industry in the United States.

As when I wrote my own job description for Mr. Grant's dealership, I was having to create many aspects of my new business on the fly. I had no idea how much to charge for this service. I had no idea how to send out an invoice or pay taxes. But I learned. I would type what the dealership owed us on a piece of paper and send it to the dealership. When they didn't pay us, I called. I was informed I had to send an invoice. What was that? I went to an office supply store and asked a clerk, who explained it to me.

Of course, Mr. Pierre was my first customer. He wished me well but urged me to go slow. Go slow? I was so excited I could have worked twenty-four hours a day. Each auto dealer to whom I pitched the program signed up immediately. I didn't hold the dealerships to any contract but just told them to try it. They all loved the results and requested that I continue.

The process I followed was the same as I'd developed for Mr. Grant. I would call the customer, thank them, get their feedback on the service given, then I would type up all this customer information and staple it to the repair order. If the customer had a complaint, I would call the service manager at the dealership, explain the problem, then leave it to him to call the customer and work things out.

Many customers were shocked to be receiving such a call. In fact, a lot of them thought it was a joke at first. This was because auto dealerships had one real focus, which was to sell cars. Once they'd talked a customer into buying a car, the salesperson would go on to the next customer, and the buyer was just abandoned. Many auto dealers felt that service departments were a necessary evil to satisfy warranties, not something that could be a profit center for their business or that keeping customers happy would ensure they bought their next car from the same dealer.

When I called to ask customers politely if they were completely satisfied, they were delighted to have someone help them navigate the system and even more astounded that a car dealership cared about them as a customer. The dealerships were soon selling more cars from the information I provided. Service managers were replaced because so many customers told stories of improper business dealings. There were positive reports as well, and those made my clients happy to have their good customer service acknowledged.

It wasn't easy, though. Every time I had to meet a new dealer and pitch our program, I felt sick with anxiety. But soon my confidence grew. I realized that this was a great service for customers and for the owners of any business. In fact, it grew so quickly that Don gave up his real estate job and joined me in this new business venture.

Customer Research, Inc., became a huge success. Over the following years, I was written up in newspapers and magazines, appeared on television, and did radio interviews. In truth, I really didn't want all that PR. I loved that no one else in the entire United States was doing anything like this, and I knew that once the word got out, the customer satisfaction industry would explode.

And explode it did. Soon Ford, Chevrolet, J.D. Power, and other auto industries all started coming up with ratings on customer satisfaction. Pretty soon, almost every business across the United States and elsewhere recognized the importance of customer satisfaction.

And why wouldn't they? God had started this entire movement with a dream. To this day, I have a magazine article framed in my office that was written about how I'd founded the customer satisfaction industry titled: *One Woman's Vision in A*

Man's Industry. The writer of that article didn't realize Customer Research, Inc. was indeed a vision given to me by God.

Today the American Customer Satisfaction Index (ACSI) is the standard by which the success of each individual auto dealership is evaluated. Ford, Chevrolet, Toyota, Chrysler, and all the other major auto manufacturers insist this type of work be done. And we were the first to eagerly fill that void. After more than fifty years, Customer Research, Inc. is still going strong led by our very talented son Dusty, who since Don and I retired has continued to take the business on to heights we never envisioned.

I love the story of Johann Sebastian Bach, an eighteenth-century composer who wrote some of the most beautiful music in the history of humanity, including the well-known Christian anthem *Jesu, Joy of Man's Desiring.* But Bach was also victim of much tragedy. Far from what we might call beautiful, his life was filled with pain. By the time he was ten, both of his parents had died. An older brother raised him begrudgingly, resentful of another mouth to feed.

Even as an adult, Bach had a difficult life. His first wife died after thirteen years of marriage. Of twenty children from two marriages, ten died in infancy, one died in his twenties, and one was mentally challenged. Eventually, Bach went blind. He was then paralyzed by a stroke.

Yet he wrote great music of profound praise, thunderous thanksgiving, and awe-filled adoration. Of German Lutheran background, Bach was perhaps the world's greatest composer of church music. Maybe it was because of the depths of tragedy he'd experienced that he also knew the heights of faith and praise.

So many people suffer very difficult life situations, but those who put their trust in Jesus Christ always seem to come out victorious. That has definitely been the case in my own life. Along with all those early years of tragedy and pain and grief, I've also been blessed beyond anything I could possibly imagine.

God blessed me with healing from a surgery where most patients die. Through Customer Research, Inc., He blessed Don and me with financial stability and abundance. He redeemed both of us, bringing us into a glorious life filled with Jesus Christ. The biggest blessing of all is to have a husband sitting by my side who loves Jesus and follows the faith and two precious sons who are strong believers.

Chapter Eighteen

Walking the Walk

I believe God's blessing is there for everyone who places their faith and trust in Him. Not only because God's Word promises such blessing (Proverbs 16:20; Jeremiah 17:7; Matthew 5:6; 2 Corinthians 9:8) but because I've personally witnessed and heard story after story of God restoring broken lives and bringing people like Don and me, who had done nothing to be chosen for God's favor, into a life of spiritual victory and joy.

We aren't unique. The apostle Paul, who once persecuted and killed other Christians (Acts 8-9), testified to his disciple Timothy how and why God reached down to save even a murderer like him.

> Christ Jesus came into the world to save sinners—of whom I am the worst. But for that very reason I was shown mercy so that in me, the worst of sinners, Christ Jesus might display his immense patience as an example for those who would believe in him and receive eternal life.
>
> —1 Timothy 1:15-16

Just like me, who better to point people to redemption than a sinner snatched from hellfire and given a second chance? Because the apostle Paul had been such a terrible sinner, his complete transformation became an even greater example of God's boundless mercy for those to whom he preached the gospel than if he'd always been a godly, righteous man. I was no renowned missionary like Paul, but I knew God was calling me to bring others to Him through my own death-to-life experience.

Still, the walk of faith isn't always easy, and the path is filled with potholes we can fall into. Maybe that's why Jesus said, "narrow is the path leading to salvation" (Matthew 7:14). Satan is constantly prowling around like that roaring lion (1 Peter 5:8), trying to get a foothold in our lives and doing everything possible to trip us up. Because of that, we can stumble and fall even after placing our faith in God and committing our lives to Him. Thankfully, our wonderful heavenly Father, Lord and Savior Jesus Christ, and God's Holy Spirit working in our lives (in other words, the Trinity!) are always there to pick us up and set us on the right path once more (Psalm 37:23-24; Proverbs 24:16; Micah 7:8; 2 Corinthians 4:8-9).

For Don and me, our life was now on an exciting path. Financially, we were doing well. Our entire family was attending church regularly.

But despite all these positive changes, the relationship between Don and me continued to be up and down. All the pain, insecurity, and self-loathing hadn't left me completely, and Don had his own scars. He and his two siblings by the same mother had spent the most time in a two-parent home since their father had stayed married to their mother until Don left for the Navy. But that didn't make for a better home life. When their father wasn't deployed at sea, he was mentally and physically abusive to his children and wife and had one adulterous affair after another.

Bottom line, we both had terrible memories and scars of abusive fathers and horrible family situations. So neither of us were prepared to be good parents, and Don was certainly not prepared to be a stepfather. He ruled the household with the harsh authority and discipline he'd learned from his father.

Meanwhile, my beautiful son Chris, who had already gone through the loss of his biological father, had been deeply traumatized emotionally and mentally by witnessing his brother being hit by a car and mortally injured right in front of him as well. I took him to counselors, but I recognize looking back that the ones I found weren't qualified to handle this broken child.

It seemed at times that the smallest thing would set off a hurricane of violent words and actions between Don and me. But the majority of our arguments centered around Chris. He was acting out increasingly. Don would discipline him, trying to *make a man* out of this broken little boy as his father had disciplined him. This tore at my heart since in my mind Chris and Mark were one. Mark was gone, and Chris was struggling in a heartbreaking way. So I would step in to protect Chris, which simply made Don even more angry and harsh toward Chris.

I won't try to justify Don's behavior, but as a very young, inexperienced stepfather in his twenties and thirties, it was difficult for him to adjust to raising a mentally injured stepson. I in turn made the horrible error of trying desperately to protect

Chris from anything in life that might hurt him. He needed to learn life's lessons, and I kept him from that. Who knows how this should have played out if Don and I had both been wiser? Coulda, shoulda, woulda—it's always easier to judge in hindsight.

What I do know is that Chris was deeply wounded and in many areas just gave up. He graduated from acting out into a life of alcohol, then heavy drugs. Many treasured things disappeared from our home to pay for drugs. We were at our wit's end, not knowing what to do.

We finally set down some rules, making clear that this was our home and we wanted him to stay with us, but he'd have to follow our rules. Instead, he chose to leave at just sixteen years old. I watched him walk up the street with his belongings in a bag, and my heart mourned the loss of yet another son.

After a few months, Chris returned home. He wanted to go into the Navy and agreed to follow our rules until he could enlist. He served six years in the Navy and came home with a Harley motorcycle. His addiction to alcohol continued, and he found his way into riding with several biker gangs. Though Don and I both dearly loved him, it was hard to watch him doing destructive things to his life.

But we never gave up on him and nor did God. After several years of heartbreaking pain, Chris joined a church that had a Christian Harley biker group. This group would go into hardened biker camps, doing dental work, marrying and burying people, and offering other assistance as needed. Being part of that ministry completely turned my son's life around.

During this same time period, Don and I both recognized faults in our parenting. Don especially grew as a godly father and apologized to Chris for the harsh way he'd step-parented him. In time they became very close. Today I'm so very proud to say that Chris is a wonderful, godly man who serves God in an exceptional way. He's a special blessing to our family, and he has finally come to know how much he is loved by his stepfather as well as his mother and brother.

As for our talented, brilliant youngest son Dusty, this incredible gift from God has been a joy since his birth and has also grown into an extraordinary man of God. Three beautiful sons, one of them already waiting for me in heaven, are truly my greatest joy. I love them more than life.

Along with parenting, Don and I still had spiritual learning to do in our marriage. Arguments over trivial matters continued to flare up from time to time. In my faith journey, I'd already learned that forgiveness was a huge part of any healing. From the night of my near-death experience, I'd wanted to forgive Don for the horrible fight we'd had in the car. We were both aware that the fight and resulting tragedy were caused by pent-up frustration and grief over Mark's death and that we'd both been at fault.

But whether or not Don hit me because he was angry or was just defending himself from my own savage assault or a bit of both, the result was that I'd literally died. Also, deep down I still carried resentment that Don had forced me out of the house to begin with when he knew how much I was still grieving. He'd allowed the argument to escalate.

And no matter what the provocation, Don and I both had been raised to believe that a man should never lay a hand on a woman in anger. Intentionally or not, for his blow to rupture my liver meant that he'd hit me with considerable force. I would forever carry the physical scar across my chest where those heroic doctors had saved my life.

I could see the guilt and remorse in Don's eyes when he looked at me. What could I say? In my heart I forgave him, and in my mind I forgave him. But Don had never verbalized any actual words of remorse and recognition of all I'd suffered. For that matter, I'd never expressed regret or asked forgiveness for having attacked him that night.

It took a long time for Don and me to come to the realization that he needed to ask me to forgive him. He needed to verbalize that he was sorry for all I'd been through. I still remember that day so vividly. We'd had an argument about nothing, as our fights usually were. Our angry conversation quickly escalated into abusive yelling.

Then I suddenly realized that I wasn't angry over whatever small point of discussion we were arguing about. I was angry with Don because of what had happened to me. The truth is that he'd suffered equally with me. I was just the one who carried the scar. But we'd never sat down and asked forgiveness from each other.

That very day, Don poured out his pain and sorrow and remorse for what had happened, then asked me to forgive him. Looking my sweet, loving husband directly in the eye, I in turn said the words, "I forgive you." We never spoke of that episode in our lives again. It truly was in the past and forgiven.

I understand now that full healing required forgiveness on my part. If I hadn't forgiven, I think I would have continued reliving the pain again and again just as though watching some movie scene on replay. That day I was able to look Don in the eye and say, "I forgive you." Only then was I able to let my anger go. I was able to extend grace to my husband just as God had extended it to me.

Jesus once said that people who are forgiven much love much (Luke 7:47). I can testify to that truth for Don and me. Our love for each other grew that day. Of course like every couple, working to keep our marriage strong is a never-ending journey. But it is one I'm very happy to be on, and even after fifty-four years of marriage, Don is still my *happy ever after.*

CHAPTER NINETEEN

NO MATTER WHAT

Forgiving God for Mark's death was a harder thing for me to overcome. I anguished in the pain of his loss for years even after having placed my faith in Jesus Christ. I found myself unable to trust God or others, so I put a circle around the lives of my remaining two sons, always walking in front of them with that net of protection. I didn't permit them to suffer the normal bumps of life and learn how to deal with pain, sorrow, failure, and other normal emotions. I became a perfectionist, and the pressure I put on my family caused many problems.

My manic state of mind did allow me to accomplish a good deal. Waking at five a.m., I would hit the ground running—literally. I ran seven days a week, trying to outrun the pain. I played tennis competitively. I took Dusty to soccer and guitar lessons, kept the house spotless, volunteered for every committee, and usually ended up running every meeting. Once I founded Customers Research, Inc., I spent many long hours at auto dealerships and automobile factories like Ford, Chevrolet, and others. I gave seminars on customer satisfaction.

One weekend, I attended a retreat at a campground north of Seattle, where I came down with some type of virus. I had a high fever and couldn't stop coughing and shivering. When I arrived home Sunday evening, I got my things ready to leave in the morning for Portland, where I had a manager meeting with the zone executives for Chevrolet Motor Division. On the two hundred-fifty-mile drive from Seattle to Portland, I chugalugged cough syrup the entire way, trying to stop my coughing.

I didn't realize the ingredients in cough syrup could cause problems similar to being under the influence if taken in quantity, and by time I walked into the room where I was to speak, my mind was completely blown. I saw a long line of black suits staring at me. I got up to speak and started by saying, "I'm Kat Dunkle, and I'm a call girl. "

Of course, what I had intended to say was that I owned a company that telephoned customers. All the male auto executives filling the room burst into hysterical laughter while I stood there in shock, wondering what was happening. When I returned to Seattle, I discovered that I had a severe case of pneumonia.

None of these things were too complicated in themselves, and I was gratified that I'd managed to accomplish so much. But eventually, it all took its toll, and my physical health broke. It all came down to the sin of pride I'd confessed flat on the floor in my white suit all those years ago as well as my continued failure to trust God. I still had the mistaken idea that I could do it all myself.

But that was a lie. I couldn't do it myself, and God showed me my failure. Seeking God's forgiveness once more, I threw myself at His feet. Once again, He was faithful to forgive, and He continued to bless me.

I wish I could say that was the last time I experienced negative emotions or failed to trust God with my life and loved ones. But the truth is that despite giving my mind, spirit, and soul to God to do with my life what He would, I remained a very imperfect sinner. I had been an atheist, and God's grace saved me. God called me to bring others to Him, and I was determined to do whatever I could to fulfill that call on my life. But it seemed like there was still a lot of cleaning up to be done in me. Of course, now I understand that I will never reach perfection until I am in God's presence and His work in me is finished as the apostle Paul reminds:

> Being confident of this, that He who began a good work in you will carry it on to completion until the day of Christ Jesus.
> —Philippians 1:6

Chronic depression was one thing I still struggled with even when life was going well in general. Physical pain can impact emotional depression as it is hard to remain upbeat when we don't feel well. The leg I'd torn apart in my water ski accident never did heal completely, leaving me with permanent nagging pain and fatigue that grew worse as the years went by. I'd always been athletic and loved the outdoors, but I felt increasingly limited, unable to participate in activities I'd once enjoyed and that my husband and sons could still experience.

One beautiful, clear winter day, I sat in church with sad news weighing heavily on my mind. All around me were faces of dear friends and hands upraised in worship. But I couldn't enter into their joy. I was often asked to pray for people, and today would be no exception. But this request hit especially close to home.

My son Dusty had received a phone call from one of his best friends. Just sixteen years old, the young man had been on a skiing trip when he felt pain in his legs. He was strong and young, so no one was too concerned. But after he returned home, the doctors ran tests and diagnosed him with bone cancer. He'd been given only a short time to live.

I knew what it was like to lose a son and was familiar with the pain this beautiful young man and his parents were going through. Gathering my troubled thoughts, I began praying for him. As I prayed, I felt God urging me to do something I knew would be very challenging. *Go lay hands on this young man and pray for him, and he will be healed.*

God's voice was clearer than any message I'd ever received from Him before, and I knew with all my being God was calling me to do this. Excited, I ran from the church and drove immediately to the hospital. In fact, it was the very same hospital where Don and I had lost our precious son Mark, so just walking through the front doors was very difficult.

I found the room where my son's friend was being cared for. A sign on the door said, *No Admittance,* but I entered anyway. My heart broke at the sight of this handsome young man lying there dying. He looked up and smiled, revealing braces on his teeth. Like my beautiful son, this teenager should be looking forward to a long, productive lifetime ahead of him, not death.

I introduced myself as Dusty's mother, then spoke to him about his need for Jesus. He said he understood and had prayed for God to come into his life. My heart pounded with excitement at this good news. I asked if he'd allow me to lay my hands on him and pray that God would totally heal him.

"Yes!" he responded. I saw a tear running down his face. This left me feeling sad that I'd made him cry yet excited that he would be healed. When I finished praying over him, I gave him a long hug and left.

Just a few days later, I received the news that the young man had died. I was so angry with God. How could He have played with me this way? Taking me to the hospital where my own precious son had died. Giving false hope to this young man. I had been obedient. I had done what I felt God calling me to do. Had it all been some cruel, heartless trick?

Day after day, I couldn't let go of the anger I felt. It flowed through me like a poison, killing everything I'd believed in. Weeks went by. Months went by. My heart just grew colder. I still picked up my Bible every morning. I still prayed for people. But now I prayed words from memory, not from my heart. I might as well have been a robot programmed to say the right thing.

For a year, I struggled with this. I was like the Dead Sea with living water flowing into it but no place for the water to go, stagnant and with no life inside. To my mind and heart, God had let me down. I can't even describe how empty and lost that made me feel, not unlike the time period after Mark's death. I longed for the days when I'd been so alive in Jesus.

Then one morning as I was praying, I heard God again. *Will you be obedient to My call? Will you follow Jesus no matter what?*

I started to cry. Falling to my knees, I trembled all over as the hold of anger and bitterness on my heart broke. "Yes, Lord, all I want is to know You. But what about the boy You sent me to? What about the promise You made that he would be healed?"

I felt God tell me not to question His ways, assuring me that He was in control, not me. No matter what the outcome, I was to obey His voice and trust Him. Even though this young man had died, he had first placed his faith in Jesus and now lived in heaven with God, whole and healed for all eternity.

In time, I have come to understand that God's perspective on healing is as different from ours as His perspective on death. The apostle Paul wrote his final letter to his disciple Timothy while on death row for his faith in Rome. God had rescued him many other times, and Paul had faith that God would rescue him again.

> The Lord will rescue me from every evil attack and will bring me safely to his heavenly kingdom. To him be glory for ever and ever. Amen.
>
> —2 Timothy 4:18

God did rescue Paul once more, but this time it was straight into heaven. And you can be sure Paul wasn't disappointed not to be returned to the battlefield. His race was completed, the good fight fought, his faith kept unwaveringly, and now it was time for him to depart for his true home (2 Timothy 4:6-8). God kept His promise to rescue Paul, just not the way his friends might have been praying for. And He'd kept His promise to heal this young man, just not the way I'd expected, for all of eternity instead of just a few more decades.

I came to realize that this was Satan's evil trickery seeking to devour me and cause me to fall away from God (1 Peter 5:8). Sadly, I lost a year of joy with my Lord and Savior. But I also gained a lot of knowledge through this experience. From that day forward, whenever I feel God urging me to do something, I do it gladly without thought to the outcome.

Well, most of the time. On another occasion, I made a hospital visit to a man on his deathbed. This man would have nothing to do with God, but his daughter was a Christian and had asked me to pray over him. When I walked into his hospital room, it was pitiful to see this shriveled, dying man who already smelled of impending death.

I talked to the man about his need to turn to God before he died, that without a Savior he'd be lost for all eternity. He seemed receptive and grateful to have a visitor. I was standing by his bed as I spoke, my hand resting casually near the oxygen lever that kept him alive. After we spoke for a while, I asked if he would like to turn his life over to Jesus.

Looking up at me, he responded, "No, I don't think I need that."

I was in shock. What did this man have to lose? He was dying, after all. I felt my hand move toward the oxygen lever, half-tempted to say bluntly, "Look, you idiot! I'm going to turn off your oxygen if you don't turn your life over to God."

I didn't tell him this because I knew the decision was his. I knew God doesn't force His way into anyone's life, and I couldn't either. Sadly, the man died the next day. As far as I know, he never placed his faith in Jesus Christ. But at least he heard the gospel before he died, so who knows if he might have repented in the end even if he never voiced his change of heart aloud. For his daughter's sake, I pray so.

Chapter Twenty

Emotions

Losing our son Mark is something that will continue to cause me mental anguish the rest of my life. In truth, few people go through life without facing grief, whether over losing a loved one, loss of a job or career, or even mourning our ability to be as mobile as we once were.

There is no way to predict how you will feel when you lose someone you love or how you will react if told you only have a short time to live. Reactions to grief are not like recipes with a list of ingredients and guaranteed results if you follow the instructions. Each person mourns in a different way. You may cry hysterically or remain outwardly controlled, showing little emotion. You may lash out in anger against your family and friends or express gratitude for their concern and dedication. You may be calm one moment and in turmoil the next. All to say, grief is universal. At the same time, it is extremely personal.

That said, there are certain stages of emotions we all tend to go through when we are grieving. And there are certain principles of healing God provides to us as we go through those stages. Maybe you have lost a loved one recently or in the past or are in the process of grieving some other painful loss. If so, I'd like to share my own emotional stages and some of the ways God helped me through them. May these lessons from God be of help and blessing to you as well.

Denial

This was one of the first emotions I felt when Mark died. I just couldn't believe this could be happening to me. I was in shock and feeling like part of me was missing. I tried to live the life I'd had before the tragedy, and when that didn't happen, I felt like a failure. I couldn't be good to myself, and any feelings of comfort or being productive simply caused guilt to rise up inside me.

Anger

Once I'd accepted that Mark wouldn't be coming back, all the unleashed anguish and pain led to the next step of anger. Anger doesn't always manifest itself as overt angry feelings. Sometimes you just become bitter or cynical. Sometimes the anger is directed at whatever terrible tragedy has occurred, but other times it is directed at yourself. You tell yourself that if you'd only been a better mother, wife, or daughter, your loved one would not have died.

Depression

I've already addressed the problem of chronic depression. Once you start blaming yourself, that of course becomes feelings of guilt and shame. All those emotions snowball into such a heavy weight that spiraling down into depression is almost inevitable. Especially if you don't seek and receive medical and emotional support.

Self-Pity

Why me? Does that statement sound familiar? Throughout my life in times of great distress, an emotion I've allowed myself to wallow in is self-pity. I was too young to remember the actual episode, but I remember well my mother telling the story of finding me in my room crying my heart out. Sitting down on my bed beside me, she asked, "Kathy, why are you crying?"

Looking up at her with swollen, tear-filled eyes, I responded shakily, "I'm just feeling sorry on myself!"

Self-pity was certainly an emotion I felt often when I was enduring an abusive marriage, rehabbing from my skiing accident, dealing with Mark's death, going through surgery, and recovering from my near-death experience.

Stress

The emotion of stress is part of everyone's life, but it becomes even more prominent when you are dealing with grief, chronic pain, or illness. Stress is a God-given emotion meant to help kick in your *fight or flight* instinct to keep you safe. But when stress is added to depression, self-pity, doctor appointments, running a business, being involved in every church function as well as school activities, various crises related to a troubled, traumatized teenager, and all the other necessities of life, the stress level becomes overwhelming.

It didn't help that I allowed others to define for me what my life should be like. Well-meaning relatives, friends, TV shows, and magazines all put unrealistic goals out there. Trying to meet all those expectations just made matters worse.

Despair

This is another emotion that can overwhelm us during our grieving. There is a little voice inside that tells us, "Why don't you just give up?" Yes, I got tired of fighting the difficulties in my life. And, yes, the easy solution would be to give up. In fact, the desire to give in to despair is what can lead to thoughts of suicide as I experienced on several occasions. But that isn't how God created us to respond. When I witness a talented artist like Joni Erickson Tada drawing with a paintbrush gripped in her teeth because she is quadriplegic, I am ashamed to have even considered throwing in the towel.

༄

I share all this to say that the path to healing isn't easy or short. There are a lot of twists and turns and two steps backward for a step forward. If people tell you that the pain and grief will be gone in days or weeks or months or even years, that is not true. That said, there is a way forward when we place our faith in a loving heavenly Father.

Prayer

I still don't have all the answers, but having gone through the loss of a child, sickness, financial ruin, and other life circumstances, I know that without submission to God and His guidance, I would not have made it. I couldn't help feeling these emotions. But spending time praising, worshipping, and seeking God's guidance in prayer brought comfort and renewed strength. God will always restore and bless us if we just turn to Him.

Bible Reading

I also spent a lot of time reading the Bible. I learned through God's Word that I have immense value to God. That worry and anxiety can melt away if I trust Him. That I can live a productive life and be victorious amidst pain. That God can use me for good even when I am still a flawed work-in-progress.

Church/Fellowship

Getting involved in a good Bible-focused church and spending time in fellowship with other Christians helped me overcome feelings of isolation and loneliness. I could also trust these Christian friends and leaders to point out when I was getting off track.

Focus

I also had to learn to invest my time and efforts wisely. This included choosing those activities I really wanted to be involved in and those without which I could live quite happily. Maybe even doing something each day that brought me enjoyment or enriched my life. I learned to be assertive about these issues when I felt I was being pushed into doing things or meeting expectations others had for me rather than what God was calling me to do.

Asking for Help

I also had to acknowledge that life just wouldn't be the same now. That I might need help during times when life threw me into illness or loss. That I shouldn't be too proud to ask others for help when I was struggling. I wanted to be there to help those who were struggling, but it did no good to ask people to know God if by my own actions I was denying Him. And that includes asking God for help and trusting that He will deliver as we read in the following two promises from God's Word.

> For he [God] will deliver the needy who cry out, the afflicted who have no one to help. He will take pity on the weak and the needy and save the needy from death. He will rescue them from oppression and violence, for precious is their blood in his sight.
>
> —Psalm 72:12-14

> So do not fear, for I am with you; do not be dismayed, for I am your God. I will strengthen you and help you; I will uphold you with my righteous right hand.
>
> —Isaiah 41:10

Surrender

Finally, I needed to make a conscious choice to surrender to God and accept what He had allowed in my life. This included the terrible loss of a loved one, the loss of hopes and dreams, even the loss and then return of my own life. God's Word tells us:

> Those who suffer according to God's will should commit themselves to their faithful creator and continue to do good.
>
> —1 Peter 4:19

For some reason, God had permitted pain to be a necessary part of my life, and I had to come to the place of surrendering into God's hands all my rage, anguish, resentment, bitterness, fear, and sense of betrayal. These were emotions that kept me from experiencing necessary healing from God. I needed to ask my Creator to walk with me through the various stages of grief and allow His love and comfort to give me renewed hope.

I also needed to recognize that God doesn't make mistakes. That there is a purpose for the way things are and who God has made me to be. That even my suffering was by God's will and for my good (Romans 8:28). The choice left to me was what to do when times got tough. Would I turn within myself or turn to God?

Whatever you are going through today, may I encourage you to make the choice to surrender to God. He loves you and desires to deliver, rescue, strengthen, help, and uphold you for you are precious in His sight. And never forget that if today may not be so good, tomorrow just might hold an unforgettable treasure of God's blessing and power as the apostle Paul reminds us from his own experience of suffering and grief:

> But we have this treasure in jars of clay to show that this all-surpassing power is from God and not from us. We are hard pressed on every side, but not crushed; perplexed, but not in despair; persecuted, but not abandoned; struck down, but not destroyed.
> —2 Corinthians 4:7-9

Chapter Twenty-One

Is It Safe to Die?

So are heaven and hell real? Was my near-death experience visiting both these places real? What about the countless other such death-to-life experiences that have been documented? I can only speak definitely to my own experience and let others speak to theirs.

One woman went through such an experience at age thirty-six during a postoperative fever of 105.5 Fahrenheit. She described feeling great joy and being surrounded by profound love and absolute peace. She felt a conviction that no harm would come to her in any way. She also sensed someone saying to her, "You're safe now. Don't be afraid. This peace will help you."

Since returning to her physical body, she has tried to recreate this peace in her mind. But she can't. Nor can she find words to describe it to others. She expresses that the depth of this feeling can't be understood unless you've experienced it yourself. But anyone who has felt this peace will never want to leave it or have it leave them.

I can certainly agree with this woman's statement. There is no description on earth that can capture this feeling of peace. But I know what it is. It is the peace of God that passes all understanding as the Bible calls it (John 14:27, 16:33; Philippians 4:7). So even though parts of my experience were negative and I heard the tortured screams of many falling into hell, I hold to that hope of peace that I believe God wants for all of us.

The truth is that hallucinations, drugs, or fevers can't explain death-to-life experiences, and they can't be recreated any more than scientists have managed to create life from inanimate matter in a lab. Yet I've found that most people reporting these experiences can reconstruct them exactly. They share astoundingly similar events, sequences, and transformations. Only around ten percent have a negative story such as mine of experiencing hell. But those who've had these experiences overwhelmingly lead remarkably transformed lives. Certainly in my own case, the entire thing scared the hell out of me literally!

Too many people reading such afterlife experiences want to focus only on the positive. To believe that there may be a heaven but not a hell. But in all things, there is a positive and a negative. An up and a down. An in and an out. And if I'm going to believe there is good, then I must also accept there is evil. If heaven is real, so is hell. In Dr. Maurice Rawling's book, *To Hell and Back: Life After Death—Startling New Evidence*, he writes:

By immunizing the public to the trauma of violence and evil, the media does encourage permissive concepts and a bland indifference concerning evil. In this way hell becomes an everyday event no longer to be feared, reducing the traditional malevolent connection with Satan. Hell has become an amusing, fun place to be, where immorality is the accepted norm.

Dr. Rawlings documented many such experiences. He goes on to say that patients who entered hell during near-death experiences were unequivocally certain that this was a real place and that they had been there. These people do not consider hell to be a deception sent from Satan. This would be counterproductive for the cause of evil. Jesus explained it this way:

> Every kingdom divided against itself will be ruined, and every city or household divided against itself will not stand. If Satan drives out Satan, he is divided against himself. How then can his kingdom stand?
>
> —Matthew 12:25b-26
> see also Mark 3:23-26; Luke 11:18

The truth is that God does exist. Heaven does exist. Hell does exist. And Satan is alive and well on this earth, always striving to divide us and pull us into eternal damnation with him. Feeling the pain of hell is something I don't expect others to understand without having experienced it any more than they can grasp the utter peace of heaven without experiencing it. But I know God brought me back for a reason. That reason was to pass on to you and others what I absolutely know now for a fact, that when people choose sin, they will suffer separation from God forever and ever and ever.

In his book *Facing Death*, the well-known evangelist Billy Graham explains that death is an enemy of God's plan. God reminds us of that through the apostle Paul.

> For he [Jesus Christ] must reign until he has put all his enemies under his feet. The last enemy to be destroyed is death.
>
> —1 Corinthians 15:25-26

When I first read this scripture passage, I wondered what that meant. Death an enemy of God? I came to understand that death destroys life in completely contrast to God the Creator and Author of life. In fact, the Bible tells us that neither sin, pain, disease, nor death were a part of God's original plan for mankind. When God created this earth and placed the first man and woman, Adam and Eve, upon it, He created everything perfect (Genesis 1-2).

Death entered the world when Adam and Eve made the choice of their own free will to disobey God (Genesis 3). God had warned them that if they ate from the fruit of the tree of the knowledge of good and evil, they would die. But Satan scoffed at God's warning and told them they wouldn't die but would instead become like God (Genesis 3:4). Adam and Eve chose to ignore God's warning and to believe Satan's lie.

Thankfully, if Satan and hell are real and the penalty of sin is death, God's love and compassion in sending His Son to pay the penalty for our sin on the cross is also real.

> For the wages of sin is death, but the gift of God is eternal life in Christ Jesus our Lord.
>
> —Romans 6:23

I have discovered that those who are most aware of their own sins also recognize how little they deserve heaven. I have given my mind, spirit, and soul to Jesus to do with my life what He chooses for me. Yet I am well aware that I can't keep from sinning and that nothing I can do would justify my going to heaven and entering the presence of a Holy God. So when I read how God sacrificed His Son to atone for our sins and yet many people reject that sacrifice, then I can understand why God allows them to fall into evil. It is part of the free will He has given human beings.

Some time ago, I was part of a volunteer team going into the only maximum-security prison for women in the state of Washington. The prison administration picked out some of the inmates to participate in a four-day retreat. Many came just to get out of lockup, but they were curious as well. I had the privilege of helping to bring God's Word and God's love to these women.

Walking between two razor-wire fences, hearing the solid steel door clanging behind you, and realizing you can't leave until the guards release you is not a pleasant feeling. I'm not sure what I expected when the participating inmates filed into the chapel. Maybe some really hardened, nasty-tempered women. After all, these women had broken the law to have ended up here.

But what I saw were women who didn't look much different than me other than the khaki-green uniform they all wore. What they most had in common was the look of overwhelming despair and misery on their faces. These women knew what it was to have their sins exposed in the light of a courtroom. They'd been locked into the midst of every form of evil and depravity.

As we became acquainted, I was moved to tears at how sin had devastated their lives and the lives of their families. They were all too eager to show pictures of their children and to speak of the loneliness of not seeing loved ones. One woman told me that no one on the outside knew she was even alive. She didn't have a single friend or family member. She was a number in a system that had warehoused her, and she wanted to take her own life. She told me that God was a forgiving God and would understand her pain in considering this self-destruction.

Even though we weren't supposed to touch inmates due to the possibility of passing off drugs or weapons, I grabbed this woman, hugged her tight, and told her my story. We cried together and prayed for God's healing touch and that she'd come to know God's purpose for her life and how even now she is valuable.

It was a good reminder to me that a vast population suffers alone locked in cells with the world going about its business and no one caring. We all sin. Some are caught and pay the price. Others of us think because we haven't been locked up for our sins that we are safe from any penalty. The truth is that we will someday be held accountable for every sin we commit, whether it's in the courtroom or to God Himself.

CHAPTER TWENTY-TWO

GOD'S GIFT OF GRACE

So if hell is a real place, will people stay there forever? I don't know. I felt I would when I fell into that pit. I certainly deserved to stay there for all I had done. But I didn't. God brought me back.

The fact is, I don't know if everyone gets a second chance to repent. But I honestly believe that loved ones who die without accepting Jesus Christ as Savior and Lord may receive the opportunity to make the right decision during their process of dying. I cried out to God as I was drawn into hell and begged to return to Him. Maybe we all get that chance.

That said, I wouldn't bet my own eternity on that, and I hope you won't bet yours if you have not yet repented of sin and accepted God's gift of eternal life.

I do believe that during the dying process God will wholly reveal Himself to us, and it will be upon that revelation that our eternity rests. Corrie ten Boom is well-known as the author of *The Hiding Place*, where she tells of her experiences sentenced to a World War II concentration camp for helping Jews escape the Nazi regime.

Her first experience with death as a young girl came from visiting the home of a neighbor who had just died. She was suddenly overwhelmed with fear and sadness over the thought that her parents would also die someday. Her father comforted her by asking, "Daughter, when we travel to Amsterdam, at what point do I give you your ticket?"

"As we're getting on the train, Father," Corrie responded.

The point Corrie's father was making is that God will give us the grace needed to face death when the time comes and not before. My mother told the story of being with her own mother when Grandma died. Grandma had been ill for some time and was bedridden. As my mother sat beside Grandma's bed waiting for her final breath, Grandma sat straight up in bed and said, "Jesus is coming for me." She then lay down and died.

I've heard and read countless such stories that are so very similar. So I do believe that something amazing happens during the dying process and that we will never be alone. No matter how violent or painful a death someone may experience, the transition into the afterlife will be a wonderful, blessed time of coming to know our God. As John the Baptist preached to the Israelites about the impending arrival of Jesus, "all people will see God's salvation" (Luke 3:6).

That said, God's grace and presence in death doesn't mean being free from sorrow when facing our own death or the death of a loved one. Nor does mourning a loss and feeling grief signify a lack of faith. That is very important to understand. Jesus wept at the tomb of His dear friend Lazarus (John 11:35) and agonized with "loud crying and tears" in Gethsemane at His own impending death (Hebrews 5:7).

Because God gave me a restored *will to live*, I really don't want to think about dying or the grief that will cause my family. But I also know the better prepared I am for that day, the easier it will be for everyone. There is nothing more important than where I will spend eternity, and I am always sad that some people don't want to talk about such important things like death and eternity.

The truth is that there are some things we will never understand. Things that God keeps secret from us, at least while we are living on this earth, as Scripture makes clear:

> The secret things belong to the Lord our God, but the things revealed belong to us and to our children forever, that we may follow all the words of this law.
>
> —Deuteronomy 29:29

> Now we see things imperfectly, like puzzling reflections in a mirror, but then we will see everything with perfect clarity. All that I know now is partial and incomplete, but then I will know everything completely, just as God now knows me completely.
>
> —1 Corinthians 13:12, NLT

Certainly, I will never understand this side of heaven the death of my precious son Mark. But the Bible reassures me that God is full of love and compassion, understanding and mercy, and that He is good (Psalm 86:15, 103:8, 145:8-9; Isaiah 30:18; Lamentations 3:22-25; Joel 2:13). Because these truths are made clear in the Bible, I must choose to believe them and to believe that whatever He has allowed in my life was necessary for His purpose to be fulfilled. If we feel crushed and brokenhearted, God is there with us.

The Lord is close to the brokenhearted, and saves those who are crushed in spirit.

—Psalm 34:18

As God reassured the nation of Israel when they were facing exile and captivity, He reassures us that He still has a plan for our lives. Not just any plan, but one of hope and a future—so long as we seek Him instead of turning away.

"For I know the plans I have for you," declares the Lord, "plans to prosper you and not to harm you, plans to give you hope and a future. Then you will call on me and come and pray to me, and I will listen to you. You will seek me and find me when you seek me with all your heart.

—Jeremiah 29:11-13

Maybe you are still asking why a loving God can allow suffering and grief to come into our lives. To put it simply, suffering has its place in God's plan. Jesus was acquainted with grief, rejected, despised, a man of sorrows who tasted death (Isaiah 53:3-10; Acts 8:26-35). And there is something about going through darkness, sickness, death, misery, hopelessness, despair, and sorrow as Jesus did that will make us be more like Him (Romans 5:3-5; James 1:2-4, 12; 1 Peter 1:6-7, 4:12-13, 5:10). One person can't really know another's pain unless they've been there themselves. True compassion requires suffering.

God has promised in the end to replace all our suffering and grief with inexpressible joy when we step into eternity (Revelation 21-22). In the meantime, we can hold on to God's promise through the apostle Paul:

For by grace you have been saved through faith, and not of yourselves, it is a gift of God, not of works, lest anyone should boast. For we are his workmanship created in Christ Jesus for good works, which God prepared beforehand that we should walk in them.

—Ephesians 2:8-10

This scripture passage tells me that God extends His grace to me. It is a gift to save me from hell, not by anything I say or do but only by God's grace. When we are in God's presence, we will each understand fully just how and why we were created. Until then, we have a responsibility to walk in the gifts that God has given us.

EPILOGUE

Well, dear reader, we have come to the end of our journey together. I would love someday to meet each one of you, if not on this earth, then in heaven, where I pray I will see you. I wrote this memoir with the goal of stirring within every reader a desire to know God in a personal way.

In my own life and family, the blessings have continued. I now have four wonderful grandchildren and two great grandchildren. They are all walking with Jesus. My sons Chris and Dusty are true believers who give credit to God for the good things in their lives. My dearest husband Don is a gentle, loving husband and father, and my love for him continues to grow each day. Markie lives on in my heart.

My sister and two brothers have all had great success in their careers. My younger brother managed several hotels before opening his own travel agency. My younger sister built a successful television career and became an ultimate athlete competing in Ironman events, cross-country skiing, and bike racing in the United States and France. As already mentioned, my oldest brother has spent most of his life in law enforcement and criminal justice.

My mother lived almost thirty years after my father died before passing away of cancer. During her last five years especially, we spent much time together, and I came to understand the difficult life she'd led. Grandma hadn't been able to care for her as a child, so my mother was raised by another family member. Later in life, she'd reconciled with her mother and gone on to become one of the first female pharmacists, only to end up trapped in an unhappy marriage with my father. We forgave each other, and her experience with Grandma seeing Jesus led her to believe my own death-to-life experience and place her faith in Jesus before she died.

Today, Don and I split our time between the warm Southern California sunshine and the cool Northwest climate of Seattle. I find great pleasure in speaking in both these regions, including at church events, for Christian organizations, and media interviews. For the past twelve years, I have also led a woman's Bible study in the Palm Springs area during the winters. I have always loved any type of sport, but due to my physical limitations I am only able to play golf, and I absolutely love doing that.

My mission continues to be bringing people to God as He directed me to do before sending me back to this life on earth. I know by God's Word that it is God who calls people to Himself. In other words, I could never cause anyone to reach out to God unless God Himself first called that person. So if you are reading these words, then know that God is calling you right now this very minute. Do you feel anything inside? Even a whisper?

If you do feel that whisper, then please do start fanning that little spark into a fire. Pray that God would speak to your heart and lead you. Pray that God would bring people into your life to guide you. Confess that you are a sinner saved by the sacrifice of Jesus Christ and give your life to God. Then sit back and hang on because you will start seeing doors open. Better than that, you have the promise of eternal life with God in heaven and not hell.

Or maybe you have already accepted God's gift of eternal life and known Jesus as your Savior. Then it is my prayer that you will take away from this book encouragement to find the good in yourself and in other people and to do your best to be what God created you to be. Please know that you are loved and very precious in God's sight. He is calling for you to know Him and walk with Him daily.

As you do so, you can indeed have absolute confidence in your heart that when the day comes it will indeed be *safe to die*. You will then go on to live for eternity with God in all His glory. All the pain and suffering and grief of loss you have known in this life will be gone, and you will live forever the wonderful promise God gives His children:

> Look, God's home is now among his people! He will live with them, and they will be his people. God himself will be with them. He will wipe every tear from their eyes, and there will be no more death or sorrow or crying or pain. All these things are gone forever . . . I [God] am making everything new!
>
> —Revelation 21:3-5, NLT

Amen! Thank you, Lord Jesus, for a life redeemed. See you there!

ABOUT THE AUTHOR

Author and speaker Kat Dunkle is the founder of Customer Research, Inc., an internationally recognized marketing and research corporation that sparked a brand-new industry of customer service in the United States. She has been the focus of many magazine and newspaper articles on women in business. She has also been interviewed for multiple television documentaries and books on her death-to-life experience, including a Netflix documentary, *Surviving Death*. She is a frequent speaker, Bible teacher, and business consultant. She has spoken and ministered with Stonecroft Ministries, Kairos Prison Ministry, Grief Share, Umbrella Ministries, Links Players International Ministry, and other outreaches. Today she lives in the Pacific Northwest with her husband Don, and enjoys spending time with her two sons and four beautiful grandchildren. Kat is committed to keep sharing as long as she is alive on this earth the command God gave her before sending her back from death to life: "Bring people to Me!" She can be contacted at thekat137@aol.com.

Made in the USA
Las Vegas, NV
19 December 2022

63639636R00105